Measuring the Impact of Training and Development on the Bottom Line

Financial Times Management Briefings are happy to receive proposals from individuals who have expertise in the field of management education.

If you would like to discuss your ideas further, please contact Andrew Mould, Commissioning Editor.

Tel: 0171 447 2210
Fax: 0171 240 5771
e-mail: andrew.mould@pitmanpub.co.uk

FINANCIAL TIMES

Management Briefings

Measuring the Impact of Training and Development on the Bottom Line

P. KEARNS

T. MILLER

FT

PITMAN
PUBLISHING

London • Hong Kong • Johannesburg • Melbourne • Singapore • Washington DC

Human Resources

PITMAN PUBLISHING
128 Long Acre, London WC2E 9AN
Tel: +44 (0)171 447 2000
Fax: +44 (0)171 240 5771

A Division of Pearson Professional Limited

First published in Great Britain 1997

ISBN 0 273 63187 X

British Library Cataloguing in Publication Data
A CIP catalogue record for this book can be obtained from the British Library.

10 9 8 7 6 5 4 3 2 1

Printed and bound in Great Britain

The Publishers' policy is to use paper manufactured from sustainable forests.

Contents

Part Two: An advanced level approach to evaluation

Appendices

Foreword

Professor Adrian Furnham, University College, London

The term 'human resources' is pronounced overhead. Human resources staff are costly, bureaucratic, unresponsive time-wasters who don't add value. Faced with the cost of training the manager is entitled to ask 'does it work'?

Professor Adrian Furnham, University College, London, *The Myths of Management* (1995).

In my experience, managers have three 'trays' on their desk, even in these times of electronic communication. They are labelled 'In', 'Out' and 'Too Difficult'. The authors of this short, but well written report address with imagination and ingenuity one of the most common problems facing the director: how to measure and hence show the efficacy of training.

Because the measurement of training has been, for many, simply too difficult, the issue has been ducked. Paul Kearns and Tony Miller are not the pusillanimous kind. They are willing, indeed eager, to confront the problem head-on with imagination. Both know this world intimately and know the literature well. The report is easy to read and very practical.

In my experience, organisations measure what they value.

Everything that exists, exists in some quantity, and can in principle be measured. Measuring employee performance at work has always been controversial. Cynics argue that what is important can't be measured, and by inference, what is (usually) measured isn't really important.

All organisations measure and monitor people, products and processes. The engineering director, the finance director and the human resources director each have their figures to present to the board. They present the statistics gathered by each department supposedly monitoring the organization. Some keep detailed records of attendance; while others would be hard-put to give even the roughest idea of either the average or individual time-keeping or sickness levels of their staff. Consider the data most organizations gather on training efficacy. Certainly all (well almost!) measure the bottom-line variables: profit, sales, costs, budget over-spend etc.

What an organization chooses to measure depends on three things; first, what type of business they are in. Organizations count, measure and audit things that seem most relevant to them; which naturally (they believe) determines success in the business. Thus, hotels measure room occupancy and airlines seats paid-for (load). Salesman firms measure revenue, profit, sales-calls, repeat business as well as mileage, customer calls and even on occasion, letters of compliment or complaint. Pubs and bars record electronically each time the server keys in an order while even academics are now measured by such things as student feedback forms, publications and exam success.

The second factor that seems important is the nature of the professionals they employ and their particular expertise. 'Bean counters' and the 'Grey Men of the bottom-line' (accountants and auditors) have been taught to count certain things in a certain way. Many become rigidly obsessed with the process and deservedly earn a negative reputation. They seem exclusively interested in measuring only certain variables, happily, even disdainfully, rejecting others. It is usually about hard variables (revenue) vs. soft (feedback forms).

Thirdly, and most importantly, organizations measure what they really value. Take, for example, specifically the Human Resource function. If one is really interested in reducing absenteeism one measures attendance; and if one is truly interested in performance appraisal one measures performance and productivity. Ask yourself the following question: what HR data does your organization hold on you? What is in the dusty manilla folder or computerized data base on you? It may contain that initial application form with all those lies you wrote about why you want to join the organization. It may have an out-of-date CV or a few rather half-heartedly completed application forms. But it is unlikely to have accurate, useful, up-to-date numerical data on your performance, skills base, aspirations etc.

Despite eulogistic disclaimers about employees being 'the most valuable asset' and managers 'really caring' about staff, it is all too apparent that organizations rarely measure staff morale or productivity. Most fall into the trap of measuring whatever can be easily measured rather than what is important. Indeed many 'quant-jocks', as my innumerate American friends call them, believe that what can't be measured really isn't very important. Or worse that what can't be easily measured doesn't really exist.

Those who resist measurement do so for ideological or incompetence reasons. The ideological resisters know that data shows up clearly individual and department differences in effort and ability. Those who favour equality (of reward) over equity like to believe that everyone is equal in terms of input and hence should be the same in terms of output. Data of practically every sort reveals this to be what it is: sentimental naivety.

The incompetent resisters to measurement do so primarily because they don't know how (not **what** to measure). Devising and putting into place robust, sensitive accurate measures is not always easy (or cheap) and takes skill. Many have tried and failed and are, as a consequence, cynical about the value of measurement. And they are often relatively skilled at shooting the messenger of measurement. They may have learnt a bit about the problems of sampling; issues of deceit, even some rudimentary statistics – just enough to confuse those eager to measure performance. But what they haven't learnt is how to evaluate performance. This report should be of immeasurable help to them.

Many managers believe in the 80/20 rule; eighty percent of sales are made by twenty percent of sales staff; eighty percent of good decisions are made by twenty percent of the managers; eighty percent of the exemplary customer service is made by twenty percent of the staff. The twenty percent need rewarding; more need selecting. But first they need to be identified by good measures. Productivity, morale, absenteeism *and* training effectiveness can be measured accurately and reliably. It takes some effort, skill and resources but it can be done – if the organization really wants the data. Some prefer not to know; others don't really care. But some do, and on the whole seem to come from more successful companies.

I recommend this report to you. It provides food for thought as well as help. The ten tool-hits are immensely useful and the case studies interesting. No-one should put training evaluation on the 'too difficult' tray after reading this report.

Adrian Furnham is Director of the Business Psychology Unit at University College, London.

About the authors

Paul Kearns

Paul's career in the human resource management field has been characterised by a determination to demonstrate how to make the people in an organisation a true source of competitive advantage. One of Paul's clients describes his ability to link human resources (HR) development to the bottom line as something akin to a heat-seeking missile.

He has developed many tools and techniques, outside of the conventional personnel and training management portfolio, which make a direct link between individual and organisational performance in bottom-line terms. This approach has redefined the role of those in the HR field who are business focused and want to add value.

Paul has been running the Personnel Works consultancy since 1991, offering a specialist service to both large, blue chip organisations and smaller businesses in the areas of HR strategy, measurement and evaluation. He has also developed a reputation as a writer and public speaker who manages to make complex subjects simple to understand and accessible for those seeking practical solutions to difficult, business-related, people issues. He is now on an Editorial Advisory Board for Croner's publications and is a specialist adviser to the Institute of Personnel and Development.

Tony Miller

Tony has spent almost all of his career in different areas of the field of training. Having worked both in the public and private sectors, in consultancy and as a specialist advisor, his contribution to this report is founded on proven successful practical experience.

His ability to achieve outstanding results from training has earned him a nickname as 'The Wizard'. He has been featured on TV and in videos as well as directing the EU video 'Training model for European success'.

Having worked as far afield as Australia, Pakistan and in almost every European country, he is able to draw from a wealth of experience. His confidence, and an ability to be able to predict and accurately measure the effectiveness of training, has enabled him to carry out large projects with a 'pay on results' methodology.

His continuing success has made him a very popular speaker on the conference circuit around Europe and internationally.

The two authors met in 1993 after they had both spent some time, independently, developing answers to the hard questions of how to measure the return on training investment. They tend to stand out from the crowd in the training and development world because, rather than exhort organisations to spend more on training and development, they are more concerned with putting a clear business case forward and seeing the returns on investment.

They share a healthy scepticism towards both the academic approach to this subject as well as the superficial rhetoric often heard from business and political leaders about the importance of training and development. Lifelong learning, for example, is one of the latest 'buzzwords' yet, without clear direction, it will never be as successful a concept as it could be.

They think the subject of evaluation is basically simple, when one looks at the practical training and development problems facing most organisations, and believe most people make it a lot more complicated than it needs to be.

They are also firm believers in the principle of 'if you cannot measure it you cannot manage it'.

Paul Kearns and Tony Miller offer a full consultancy and support service to organisations seeking to achieve the maximum return from their training investment. They can be contacted at:

Personnel Works
PO Box 109
Westbury on Trym
Bristol
BS10 5BF

Telephone: (0117) 950 7917
Fax: (0117) 950 7891

Some interesting quotes on measurement

The importance of measurement has been recognised by many business writers, and others, for a long time. Unfortunately, though, acceptance of measurement as a management tool appears to have been met with a distinct lack of interest from those responsible for training and development investment decisions. So, in order to make the point that measurement is a **must**, here is a selection of quotations that are particularly relevant to training and development:

Measure what is measurable and make measurable what is not so.

Galileo Galilei (1564–1642)

You can't manage what you don't measure.

Peter Drucker

Measurements are key. If you cannot measure it you cannot control it. If you cannot control it you cannot manage it. If you cannot manage it you cannot improve it.

Dr James Harrington
(from *Business Process Improvement*, McGraw-Hill, 1991)

If you don't measure it you're just practising.

Robert Galvin (ex Chief Executive Officer, Motorola)

If you don't measure it people will know you're not serious about delivering it.

James Belasco, *Teaching the Elephant to Dance* (Century)

When it comes to measurement and evaluation, there still seems to be more talk than action. HRD executives admit there are few bottom-line ties to their training efforts.

Dr Jack J. Phillips, *Measuring the Return on Investment*,
American Society for Training and Development, 1994

It would be very difficult to take issue with any of these views but training and development seems to have managed to avoid facing up to the issue for so long. But for how much longer? Look at this quote:

Nestling warm and sleepy on your company like an asp in Cleopatra's bosom is a department who spend 80% of their time on routine administration. Chances are its leaders are unable to describe their contribution to value added apart from trendy, unquantifiable terms. Yet this department frequently dispenses advice on how to eliminate work that does not add value. I am, of course, describing your human resources function, and have a modest proposal. Why not blow the sucker up?

Thomas A. Stewart, *Fortune* Magazine, January 1996

This report aims to firmly grasp the nettle. It will then be up to you to decide whether to stick with your existing approach to training and development, fundamentally change it, or blow it up and start again.

Part One

Getting the Basics Right

1 Introduction

Is Training a Good Thing?

One long-standing joke about how much companies spend on advertising goes something like this – 'Half the money we spend on advertising is wasted – the only problem is, we don't know which half!' The same criticism could be applied to investment in training and development.

This may be rather disconcerting for an individual company, but when one considers the billions of pounds spent on training every year in the UK, and assumes that half of it is wasted, that is an awfully large amount of money down the drain and some evidence to date suggests that it may even be worse than we think.

This report is an attempt to start to provide some answers to this particular problem. It addresses such questions as 'what makes training pay?' and 'how much of a return on investment can be achieved?' But it also raises the secondary questions of 'could we get a better return on this investment elsewhere?' and 'can we achieve the same return more cheaply?'

What is amazing is that **real** interest in evaluating the bottom-line benefits of training and development has only started to surface in recent years. This does not mean that there is no literature on the subject. Quite the contrary. Academic and professional books abound and hardly a month goes by without some reference to this question being raised in business journals. Also, the conference industry manages to attract audiences to hear from people who 'have the answer' but can produce little evidence to prove it. So, unfortunately, it appears to be a topic that has been peculiarly resistant to the discovery of practical solutions.

Paradoxically, despite the conspicuous lack of any convincing, hard evidence that training and development makes any significant difference to organisational performance, there appears to be universal agreement that training and development is crucial to organisational effectiveness!

The public pronouncements on the importance of training and development more often sound like a religious mantra rather than clear-headed commercial sense – and woe betide anyone who dares to suggest otherwise. Well, this report dares.

Saying training is a good thing to do, period, is nonsense. It *can* be good when it is designed to achieve clear objectives and delivers what it promises;

but without clear objectives it can become a very expensive waste of not only time, money and effort but, perhaps even more importantly, also the individual trainee's commitment and motivation.

But this simple fact of life never looms very large in most of the training literature or even in the sort of documentation dispensed to those wishing to achieve Investor in People (IIP) status.

Yet, if we include education alongside the broadest definition of training and development, then it could be said that it is now well towards the top of the economic, social and political agenda. Moreover, it will stay there now until such time as we are truly convinced that we are getting it right. So what criteria could be used to convince organisations to maintain investment in training and development? This report tries to provide some indicators.

A Significant Breakthrough in Evaluation Models

Anyone who has already researched some of the existing literature on this subject, and wants to see some tangible results from training, will probably feel very disappointed and frustrated by the failure of the evaluation literature to really get to grips with the practical issues surrounding evaluation.

In short, this is because the evaluation models do not define evaluation properly and then compound the crime by not working in practice! (This will be covered more fully in Chapter 4.)

The **KPMT model**, developed by the authors and used in this report, is believed to be the first significant breakthrough in evaluation since the late 1950s when Kirkpatrick introduced his own simple, but rather limited, four-level model.

To justify this claim, some time is spent on illustrating, in very simple terms, how the KPMT model is conceptually and practically superior to any other model currently in use.

Why a Toolkit?

A great deal of effort, particularly since 1994, has been focused in the area of devising evaluation tools and techniques, particularly for small and medium sized enterprises (SMEs), because they do not normally have professionally qualified training staff. But even in well-established training departments it is quite clear that they do not have the requisite tools and techniques to really evaluate the benefits of their efforts.

Therefore, practical help in the form of a 'toolkit' is a genuine attempt to offer readers something they can take from this report and try out in their own workplace – although it should also be stressed that the text of the report itself is designed to provide a framework and conceptual basis for using the tools.

However, providing a set of high-quality tools does not make someone a craftsman overnight. So the tools and techniques here must be practised, and hopefully mastered, over a period of time, if any serious attempt at evaluation is to be made.

How the Report is Structured

This is not a report about validation methods. The authors believe that true evaluation can only take place on two levels. Some training is relatively easy to evaluate (such as sales training) but such obvious situations rarely occur in practice.

Often, there are a whole host of complex variables involved which makes most training and development resistant to simple evaluation models. Consequently, there is a more advanced level offered, here, for those who regard themselves as past the beginners stage in evaluation terms.

The report is intended to form a coherent whole, but it is broadly subdivided into:

- putting training and development in context;

- covering the theory of evaluation by reference to various models;

- offering a proven, and established, practical model (KPMT);

- creating an appreciation of the importance of a strategic approach to training and development;

- specific, practical tools and techniques, some of which can be used in practice very quickly, to apply the theory at work;

- case studies showing how the tools have already been used successfully.

Where Are You Now in Training and Development?

But before you move on it is very important to consider the baseline from which you are starting. If you are not very competent at evaluation, then this report should be of immense value. But even if you are already practising evaluation at a reasonable level, then there should also be some key learning points here.

Where is your business in terms of its evolution? Is it new, in a mature market, leading edge, facing tough competition? How much training and development does your organisation undertake consciously? If you do little training now, then maybe there are many improvement opportunities awaiting you.

If you already 'do a lot' of training the issues are different – what works and what doesn't? Is all training and development just a list of pick-your-own standard courses or are you moving towards self-development, or even aiming at becoming a learning organisation?

If you want to be a learning organisation then you may find the advanced section particularly useful to find even further improvement.

You could actually move now to Tool Number 1 to try and obtain a clearer picture of where you currently stand in training and development, before you start to work your way through the rest of the report.

2 The changing business case for investing in training and development

Why Evaluation Has Come to the Top of the Agenda

In 1989 a Training Agency survey showed that less than 3% of companies were carrying out any formal cost-benefit analysis of training spend.

Research headed by Professor David Storey of Warwick University (*Understanding the Small Business Sector*, Routledge, 1994) indicated that, despite a belief by the Confederation of British Industry (CBI) and the Department of Trade and Industry (DTI), that training and development was an important factor in company performance, there was no evidence to support this view. Some of the researchers on the project from Newcastle University stated that:

> *The lack of a clearly demonstrable link between training and firm performance is one of the reasons why many firms are reluctant to invest in human resources.*

Needless to say this was not what the CBI or DTI had expected, or wanted to hear, and the CBI immediately set up a working group to look at the matter.

A survey of 500 firms by the Industrial Society in August 1994 showed that business efficiency was cited by 75% of the sample as the reason for evaluating training. The report issued with the survey results stated:

> *... economic pressures have simply made it increasingly vital for employers to tighten up spending on training cash.*

The second most important factor in this survey (cited by 45% of respondents) was the need to evaluate as part of the Investors in People (IIP) standard.

These are just a small selection of statistics which indicate what little effort has gone into evaluation in the past and why it is now seen as so important.

Certainly, in recent years, cost reduction and relentless pressure to improve organisational performance have had a part to play in moving evaluation up the agenda. However, total quality management, as a philosophy, could be said to have had the greatest influence on this because continuous improvement means having a total quality system and at the heart of any **total quality system** is the need for measurement.

As indicated in the measurement quotes on page xv of this report, there have always been plenty of well-respected writers who have emphasised why measurement is so important, but this pressure has been resisted by the training and development function for so long. Some have tried to argue that it is unmeasurable, some have said it is unnecessary and others are just simply afraid of it!

Alternatively, some training professionals now say they are not 'training employees' but acting as agents, or facilitators, of learning. This is a particularly clever escape clause.

Yet recognition of the need for, and the importance of, measurement has never gone away.

Perhaps one reason why training and development has managed to ignore evaluation is that, when the total quality revolution started, there were just so many obvious improvements in operational targets to aim at that training and development managed to keep out of the spotlight.

But when the big, step improvements have already been achieved, and easy targets no longer present themselves, the focus of attention starts to move around to any other areas of cost or investment which have not been subject to the rigorous discipline of a total quality methodology.

Not surprisingly, the main interest in evaluation seems to be coming from businesses where margins are extremely tight (hotels, leisure) or product differentiation is difficult (financial services) and therefore every last drop of improvement is constantly sought.

Also, although training and development has been very much under the spotlight for the last five years or so (particularly since IIP was launched in 1991), progress has been slow because of the absence of a practical approach to evaluation which looks at business measures.

Before we move on, though, it is worth pointing out that it is not just small companies that do not spend much time on evaluation. For many large organisations, with well-established training and development departments, very little validation or evaluation has been taking place, other than the use of post-course questionnaires (pejoratively known as happy sheets), and even for them it is a relatively new area of expertise that they are trying to develop.

Yet, even without evaluation in place, it appears that some organisations did not reduce training spend during the last recession. This is often quoted as a vote of confidence in training and development without anyone stopping to consider exactly what level of service or quality of output is being delivered.

Reasons for Getting Evaluation Right

So, while it is relatively easy to see why evaluation is becoming important, from the organisation's point of view, are there any other reasons why time and effort should be put into evaluation to make sure you get it right?

Ironically, evaluation of training becomes a particular issue when someone in the organisation, at a sufficiently senior level, starts to ask what the benefits of all the training activity are. If this is the case, then it would suggest that it is not blatantly obvious how training is currently linked in with business performance or even what it is trying to achieve in business improvement terms.

This is a very difficult starting point for anyone new to evaluation because it means, in practice, that some attempt has to be made to justify training which has already taken place. Unfortunately, in such circumstances, it is highly unlikely that business measures will **already** be in place to demonstrate a payback on training and development spend.

This is a real problem for those organisations which run menus of courses because they now have to find links between these off-the-shelf courses and some business improvements that may have resulted. This can be a very time-consuming task which is often, ultimately, frustrating because it is usually extremely difficult to establish any links between training and business performance *after the event.*

For those who find themselves in this predicament, a closer look at this problem will be taken in Chapter 7 and some simple ideas are suggested which might help.

Despite any immediate hurdles that might present themselves, there are several very sound reasons for starting to put more effort into evaluation. Evaluation:

- is about building credibility and a solid foundation for training and development investment decisions;

- provides a basis for maximising return on investment;

- helps to categorise training by the type of return you will get from your investment;

- for those who get it right, should lead to building up the training function, not depleting it;

- automatically links training and development with strategic and operational business objectives;

- ensures buy-in and commitment at all levels;

- produces results that can act as a great reinforcer of learning and further motivate individuals to develop themselves.

But to obtain all of these benefits, the first step is to try and make all your training and development activity very business focused.

3 Business-focused training and development

What Is 'Training and Development'?

This is not an academic book but the question of what exactly is 'training and development' is probably a more valid and pertinent question now than it has ever been.

Allied to this question is the equally important one of where does training and development fit with the overall running of the organisation? Is it just something that happens as a reactive answer to an immediate business need (for example, the newly promoted manager who has to go on a presentation skills course) or is it planned well in advance, and totally integrated with the business strategy and operating plans, as fully intended by the Investor in People standard?

The perception of training as 'courses' is deeply ingrained in the minds of many managers, both in terms of their own formative training and development experiences over the years, as well as how they perceive 'training' for their own staff. This is not helped by the fact that, what little effort has gone into evaluation in the past has tended to focus on the evaluation of specific, discrete training courses rather than any broader, ongoing development activity.

Also, the growth of training 'departments' can foster the notion that training and development is something *detached* from the business and operating outside of it.

Even worse still, it can lead to the sort of views that training and development is something 'done to' or inflicted on people or, alternatively, that it is just a pleasant break from the pressures of everyday working life. All of these perceptions create an atmosphere in which it will be difficult for effective, business-focused training and development to take place.

An interesting anecdote from Frizzell, an insurance company, illustrates how much training functions have to avoid the wrong perceptions of training and development being created. One of the authors of this report was once asked by a work colleague if his department could help to organise a corporate 'fun day'. He refused, very politely, but very firmly. He was absolutely sure that this was no more a job for the training function than it was for the finance department. The credibility of the function can easily be eroded by such requests. He would not even lend them any of the department's equipment which was designed for teambuilding exercises.

If you want to take training and development seriously, perceptions are very important. Training and development is about achieving business results or it is nothing.

Yet training and development can include many, many other activities and initiatives which may not immediately be perceived as such. First, there is the whole area of **coaching**, **mentoring** and even **counselling** of an individual by their own manager or by someone else appointed to the task.

On-the-job development could be seen as taking place every day and is likely to be amongst the most effective methods of learning.

What about **quality improvement teams**? Are they just operationally focused teams or do they, in themselves, provide an excellent platform for continuous development of employees?

Admittedly, some specific training programmes may be run to help launch and promote quality improvement teams and efforts may be made to evaluate their contribution to team performance. But actually forming such teams in the first place could be seen as a developmental tool worthy of evaluation.

Learning and Self-Development

So, if real progress is to be made on this subject, it is important to stop looking at training and development as something which is 'done to people' and move towards a notion of what they can get out of training and development, that is, learning. Moreover, it is learning that can help to improve both their own performance and that of the organisation.

Also, the measurement of training that has been used in the past often never went any further than course costs, numbers of training days or the number of people who have attended a course.

Such measures are, at best, looking at possible training **inputs** (there is no guarantee that they are true inputs if, for example, the money is not spent wisely) and tell us nothing of the **outcomes** (the actual learning taking place) or the **outputs** (the effect this learning is having on the business). For example, 100 man-days of sales training courses is not even a guarantee that the participants have learnt anything, never mind improved their selling skills or increased sales.

Again, without getting too deep into the psychology of learning or learning styles, how people learn is very personal to them. How much they learn and at what speed can be dependent on so many factors covering everything from personal motivation to capability and attitude.

Pouring 'training' into people does not guarantee anything in return, especially if you do not explain to them why they are being trained and how it will affect their contribution to the business. So we need to focus on outcome and organisational outputs when we start to consider what it is we have to evaluate. Only by doing so will training and development start to become business focused.

Moving Away from Seeing all Training as Good

Taking this type of argument one stage further, it is quite clear that certain types of training are absolutely crucial in most organisations. There is a wide range of training tasks that have to be undertaken as an absolute minimum. Without such training the organisation would not be able to function at a level, or to a standard, that it deems absolutely necessary. A direct selling insurance company has to train its operators how to answer the telephone correctly. Even the simplest production task, packing parts in boxes, involves someone being trained how to do it. These simple principles apply throughout every level in the organisation.

But that is, more or less, the end of the story. Basic or initial training (induction, health and safety, product knowledge) is a relatively straightforward task which is unlikely to cause too many headaches – as long as it is kept to a standard and delivered cost effectively. If such training can be clearly defined, there is little point in trying to evaluate the benefits when the consequences of *not* doing the training, or getting it wrong, are so obviously detrimental.

But how much of existing training and development activity is not absolutely necessary? It is only when this question is asked that we can start to focus on the other broad category of training and development, which is training and development that is not just intended to support the existing operation but is more focused on added value – both now and in the future (a definition of added value and a fuller discussion is provided in Chapter 4).

Training can only bring added value results if there is an opportunity for added value. Either the business is not performing effectively because people are not performing, or there is a market opportunity which can be exploited but requires some new training or development.

In an established organisation, or in a mature market, many obvious opportunities will already have been exploited. Margin improvement will have been squeezed to such an extent that there are few opportunities left for step improvements. This is a fact of life but it does not seem to stop organisations throwing money at training in the vain hope that it will automatically bring some benefits.

In a new, young or rapidly changing market, then, the speed at which the organisation can react or anticipate the changes will offer a different set of opportunities for training and development.

Here, we start to see why the notion of the learning organisation is so attractive. Another definition of the learning organisation is the 're-adaptive' organisation which should be self-explanatory.

Training as Cost Versus Training as Added Value

If training and development can be broadly split into the two categories suggested, basic and added value, it is relatively easy to see why the measurements used will tend to be quite different for each.

Basic training *has* to be undertaken, but checks must be made that it is working, that is validation measures should be put in place (e.g. are the boxes being packed properly?). If you are satisfied that the training is working, this only leaves the questions of can the individual be trained to the required standard more quickly and at a lower cost?

Measurements in these areas will ensure that training delivery is being achieved as cost effectively as possible.

With added value training, however, whilst the two questions above are equally important, the *most* important question now is 'does the training really deliver added value to the business?' In other words, if the organisation does not depend on this type of training for survival, is it worth doing it at all? What is the payback, both in absolute terms and relative to the return that could be obtained by spending the money elsewhere?

This is the key question that this report is trying to answer.

Can Poor Training and Development Damage the Business?

But before we move on, let us explode one myth. Although more and more people are coming to accept that not all training is necessarily 'good', there still seems to be a perception that training does not normally do any harm. If this is your understanding then it is a very dangerous assumption.

We will look later at how training can so easily fail (see Tool Number 7) but we ought also to consider the damage that poorly designed or poorly delivered training and development can cause.

Let us take as an example one area of personal effectiveness training – assertiveness.

Is being more assertive a good thing? It might be for somebody who is talented or very capable, but cannot assert themselves enough in meetings to get their view accepted. What about someone who is not so capable. While they are unassertive they are likely to do less damage than if they suddenly start to express their opinions more forcibly after attending an assertiveness course!

Equally, in the broader area of management development, when is a manager fully developed, and is a partially developed manager better or worse than an undeveloped manager? There is some truth in the old saying that a little knowledge can be worse than no knowledge at all.

At a time when the focus of development is on managerial competencies it could be argued that developing specific competencies could alter the overall balance of managerial performance adversely. Also, some competency lists include 'initiative', 'drive' and 'judgement'. These probably *are* some of the traits that really distinguish high performers from average performers but can they be developed in an individual that does not possess them naturally?

These are big questions and cannot be answered here but they are raised now to emphasise the point that some evaluation must take place if we are to feel confident that our training and development activity is having the desired, positive effect both on the individual and the organisation as a whole.

Training Needs Analysis

Business-focused training and development starts from a business-focused training needs analysis (or TNA, sometimes referred to as an 'identification of training needs' or ITN).

The success or otherwise of any training and development activity is going to depend, to a very great extent, on the ability of those designing training events to accurately analyse the training needs of the organisation and the individuals in it. Poor analysis will inevitably lead to poor design and low value delivery.

There are many texts on TNA. Some have quite useful algorithms to lead the analyst, systematically, through a review of all the considerations which will result in identifying what training is necessary. The better algorithms start with an assessment of what business needs exist, before actually starting to look at training needs.

However, the crucial step of moving from clearly identified business needs to business focused training and development needs, involves the analyst having developed their own, high level, skill set to make this process work properly.

Let us assume that one business need, explicitly stated in the business plan, is to achieve a 10% improvement in sales in the coming year. What training and development needs does this imply? Would it be valid to automatically assume that some sales skills training would have to take place? If the business plan was constructed on the premise that a 25% increase in advertising spend would achieve the desired 10% increase in sales then maybe no additional sales training is required. (See Tool Number 3 to see how business needs can be broken down and simultaneously linked to training needs.)

Just this very simple example should highlight the fact that there could be many other ways of increasing sales turnover by 10% (e.g. launching a new product or even just putting up the price), each of which may dictate a very different set of training needs.

Even at the simplest level, training and development can be a very complex operation. That does not mean to say it has to be complicated – this is a crucial distinction which is often forgotten in common parlance.

For now, let us just acknowledge that this early phase of training needs analysis is a critical step in attempting to maximise the bottom-line impact of training and development and, as such, should command a great deal of time and effort.

Often, in practice, organisations rush into very expensive training programmes without having spent sufficient time on the analysis phase. A good example of this was the company which was so proud of a £2 m training programme that it submitted it to a National Training Award selection panel, only to have it rejected because the panel could see no business reason for designing the programme in the first place.

The use of total quality systems (TQS) thinking will become apparent throughout this report and the basis of any effective TQS has to be a plan based on an accurate analysis of what is required.

Just before we leave this section, though, let us consider how development needs analysis might take place. It is not surprising that trainers often want to run courses that, at least, appear to be offering something tangible such as sales skills, but it is not so easy to offer a course in the less tangible world of development.

When a sales person has all the sales skills they need, what other development needs might they have? To become an effective sales manager, who no longer sells directly, they now have to achieve sales targets through the skilful management of their sales people.

This leads us deeper into the muddied waters of management development and competencies. The question that needs to be asked, therefore, is can a clear distinction be made between training needs and development needs? An answer to this question will be attempted in the advanced section of Chapters 8 to 10.

Training and Development as Part of a Business Process

Part of the answer to the problem of directly drawing out training and development needs from the business plan is to install a training and development process that is linked to the way the business operates.

Figure 3.1 is a graphical representation of the process for annually reviewing training and development at Frizzell. It is important to note that this is a quality system with inputs from several angles (directors, managers) and a crucial part of the system is evaluation and a feedback loop.

This process is ideally suited to the quality system requirements of the Investors in People framework and has been recognised as such in two successful assessments for the standard.

Over a period of time, probably some years, the discipline of linking training and development to the business in this systematic way, and constantly reviewing its effectiveness, is the best way to ensure that training and development remains business focused at all times.

At a higher, strategic level the links can become more difficult to make but we will address this in Chapter 10 (and see also Tool Number 9).

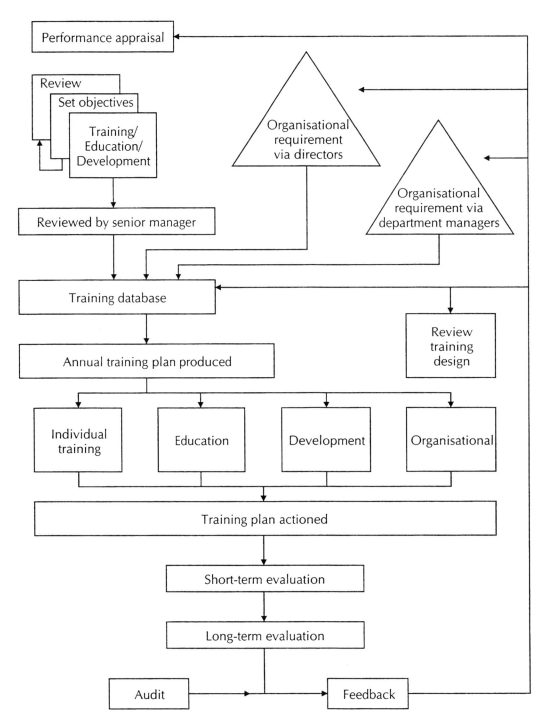

Figure 3.1 Training and development as part of a business process.

4 Choosing an evaluation model

Why Do You Need a Model?

Some of the main reasons include the following.

- Evaluation is measurement and no measurement can take place, with confidence, without an agreed, consistent approach. The model is meant to provide such consistency.

- Training is a process involving many people including the trainee, trainer, manager and colleagues, and evaluation requirements must be understood by everyone. Otherwise, all those involved will use a different basis for judging the benefits from training and development.

- Similarly, having a model shows everyone where they fit into the process and how it adds value to the business.

- Measurement has to be systematic and use a yardstick. The ultimate yardstick has to be business performance. The model should build this in.

- Training and development covers a wide range of activities so we need some basic principles that are flexible enough to be applied to any of them. The principles will be enshrined in the model.

- If training and development is not working, the model should point you in the direction of where the problems are occurring. A model normally covers several sequential steps, checking at each stage that the training is or is not effective.

So it is relatively easy to see that, before you can even begin to evaluate training and development, you must adopt an evaluation model – usually consisting of several discrete steps relating to different parts of the learning process.

Whatever model is chosen, it should be robust enough to be applied both to straightforward, easily measured training – such as training production operators to spot errors in parts on the production line – as well as developmental interventions which are less amenable to clear measurement. It should also be flexible enough to adapt to different training methods (formal course, self-development, etc.).

What Models are Available?

On an Institute of Training and Development (ITD, now merged into the Institute of Personnel and Development) certificate course that one of the authors of this report attended in 1986, the subject of evaluation arose and the lecturer intimated that evaluation was easy enough for operator training but that no one really had any clear idea how to evaluate management training. The subject was left hanging in the air because it was regarded, at best, as problematic, and, at worst, impossible. This is typical of earlier views on evaluation.

Interestingly enough, there are many models available to choose from, although a high proportion of these are just variations on a theme. Unfortunately, most tend to focus on the evaluation of 'courses' – probably because of the problems acknowledged by the lecturer on the ITD course.

The most commonly quoted model is that developed by Dr Kirkpatrick over 30 years ago. At the time, it was regarded as being at the cutting edge but now it is less appropriate for the full spectrum of training and development activity.

According to Kirkpatrick's observations, training and development can be validated and evaluated on four basic levels. His model can be summarised as follows:

Level 1   –   Reaction

> Most commonly measured by using happy sheets.

Level 2   –   Learning

> Tests can be given to check that participants learned something.

Level 3   –   Transfer of Behaviour

> Are the participants using what they learned on the programme back at work?

Level 4   –   Organisational benefits

> Did the training and development initiative have any impact on the business itself?

But before we move forward, it is worth just pausing for a second to consider this fact. If any of the existing models worked, why is evaluation still such a thorny problem?

It is barely credible that everyone using the Kirkpatrick model has not been using it correctly, so we have to conclude that there is something inherently wrong with the model itself.

It is very easy to see why the Kirkpatrick model, as it stands, does not work in practice. For example, if we send someone on a sales training course the effectiveness of the training input could be measured at Levels 1, 2 and 3.

When Level 4 is reached, however, in order to show the difference that it made to the business, we would have had to have measured the pre-course sales performance (£X thousands per annum) and then measured the post-course figure (£Y thousands per annum). The evaluation measure would then be, crudely, Y minus X. If there was no measure of X in place *before the course started*, then it would be impossible to carry out this evaluation calculation after the course.

This is a very simple point but is one that even the Investors in People framework fails to emphasise.

There are four key principles in the IIP standard and evaluation just happens, unfortunately, to be number 4. Therefore, it leads many organisations to leave it until last. By which time it is too late.

Kirkpatrick also suffers from other fatal flaws but we will come to a fuller critique of the model later. Now let us look at a representative sample of some of the many other models in use, to see if they are any better.

The Endless Belt of Development Model

Like Kirkpatrick, this model looks at a series of steps towards evaluation:

Stage 1   –   Recognise a business need

Stage 2   –   Define development objectives

Stage 3   –   Design learning process

Stage 4   –   Experience the learning process

Stage 5   –   Use and reinforce learning

Stage 6   –   Judge the benefit to the organisation

This model, used by several organisations, including Rover, looks much more up to date. It is a definite move away from just measuring 'training courses', preferring to focus instead on learning.

It also *starts*, quite clearly, with 'recognising a business need' which Kirkpatrick fails to do.

However, when Stage 6 is reached it refers to 'judging' the benefit to the organisation. This suggests that the business need, supposedly already recognised at Stage 1, was not measurable in hard terms.

The CIRO Model

The CIRO model takes its name from the initial letters of the following:

Context evaluation

Input evaluation

Reaction evaluation

Outcome evaluation

It is probably one of the more sophisticated approaches to evaluation and deserves some greater attention, not only because it is a very comprehensive view of where training analysis should start from, but also because it covers a much broader perspective than the simple Kirkpatrick model.

Its main deficiency, though, is its failure to define value – and hence evaluation – in clear and precise terms. The term 'reaction evaluation', which can only ever be a form of validation, undermines what is otherwise a useful model because it reduces its emphasis on the importance of added value, which is the only true measure of bottom-line impact.

The Institute of Employment Studies Model

The Institute of Employment Studies (IES, formerly the Institute of Manpower Studies) produced a report (*Measuring the Effectiveness of Training*, M. Spilsbury, IES Report 282, 1995) which describes a model that has been 'synthesised from various different types of cycle and takes account of all the major steps'.

This starts with:

Stage 1   –   Identification of training need:
'Examining what skills and attributes are necessary for the job to be undertaken, the skills and attributes of the job holder and the extent of the gap.'

and at:

Stage 5   –   Evaluating the effects of the training on the organisation

it adds that: '...This is the area in which there is perhaps the most confusion and subsequently little real action in the workplace'. (!)

For what is a very recent study, it shows a remarkable lack of awareness of the broader issues of 'development' and as a hybrid model, which has no chance of being able to evaluate the impact of training on the organisation, because it does not start from bottom-line measures.

Why Most Existing Evaluation Models Don't Work in Practice

We could look at many other models but most, if not all, of them suffer from some very simple but fundamental flaws. Not only are they conceptually flawed but they are virtually unworkable in practice. The most common problems include the following.

- First, they start from the wrong point, or they don't emphasise enough that evaluation begins at the start, not the end, of the training cycle.

- Second, they start with a training need, not a business need.

The IES model actually shows the first step as 'skills and attributes of the job' but how do you determine what skills and attributes are required? Multi skilling and flexibility mean that this is not a simple question and the skills and attributes of managerial jobs are not easily sub-divided.

As we discovered in Chapter 3, the training needs analysis stage of the **evaluation** process is crucial and it must link in with business needs. It is impossible to start with skills and attributes without first asking 'what skills and attributes are needed to ensure the business operates as cost-effectively as possible.'

This simple but fundamental point is recognised in the endless belt model because it starts with the question 'recognise a business need'. But what exactly does that mean?

Would the statement 'we need better management skills' be a statement of a clear business need? Well, it could be a valid conclusion that the organisation does indeed need to improve its management capability.

However, the questions get very difficult when you have to ask which managers need which skills and how will we know when they have those skills.

The answer to these imponderable questions is in the original business analysis. Poor business performance may have led to the conclusion that management capability was lacking. But poor performance, itself, is measurable and can be attributed to particular areas of business operation.

For example, let us assume that current cost levels are X% higher than originally allowed for in the business plan. One of the reasons for the high costs could (surprise surprise!) be due to lack of effective cost controls. These, in turn, could be due to particular managers not controlling costs or not putting in place a cost control system or mechanism.

So 'recognise a business need' means having a measurable business problem (the gap between planned costs and actual costs incurred), which it has been decided can be improved through better management training and/or development. We will come later to the question of whether this conclusion is valid or not and whether there could equally be a non-training problem that must be addressed.

Using this example it should be relatively easy to see that the original statement:

- could be expressed very clearly in business terms (we need an X% improvement in costs);

- will apply differently to different managers;

- will, therefore, imply different training and development needs in each case (some may need to be more assertive in cost control and others may need to understand cost control systems).

So, a 'good' evaluation model must start from a clearly identified, measurable, bottom-line business need. Moreover, the model should constantly emphasise the importance of getting this first step right.

The next – and biggest – stumbling block in virtually the whole of the available literature on evaluation is that there is a fundamental distinction to be made between evaluation and validation. Yet most models confuse validation and evaluation.

Validation will tell you whether the training achieved its training objectives but will tell you nothing about the effect it is having on the business. So validation measures on a financial spreadsheet course might say something about whether the participant enjoyed the course, what they learned about spreadsheets and, maybe, whether they actually went back to work and used them in practice. What they will not say is whether the course improved financial management in the organisation to such an extent that it improved return on capital or profit.

Evaluation, however, is a measure of the **value added** by the training and development. In other words, evaluation is saying how much effect training and development is having on the bottom line. Added value is a perfect definition of value for evaluation purposes because it:

• 	takes into account cost and benefit simultaneously;

• 	is very measurable in hard, monetary terms;

• 	is what everyone in the organisation should be focused on anyway and makes training, therefore, much more integrated with business operations.

Also, the more conventional models seem to refer to training courses only. This is not actually true of all other models although, in practice, it is usually only courses which seem to attract much attention when it comes to evaluation. One great advantage of the endless belt model is that it is so focused on the notions of development and learning rather than just courses.

In fact, when the advanced approach to evaluation becomes clear it will be apparent that, outside of technical or knowledge-based training, courses do not seem to offer a particularly cost-effective method of training or development.

Finally, the models do not fully take into account the fact that training can fail so easily. Training is generally seen as a good thing to be doing and the models above are just trying to work out 'how good?' They do not cater for the possibility that training and development can completely fail. Tool Number 7, discussed later in this report, shows just how easy it is for training interventions to fail.

If this is not enough evidence to illustrate why so little progress has been made in evaluation, there are other problem areas that need to be brought into the discussion.

Soft and Hard Measures

One of the greatest potential stumbling blocks in evaluation is the distinction so often drawn between what are usually called 'soft' measures and 'hard' measures.

As with many distinctions, it is more apparent than real. A training manager in a civil service organisation, recently moved into the training function from an operational role, referred to some of his new colleagues in 'management development' as 'luvvies'. The implication was that they saw their role as something quite different to delivering hard results for the organisation.

Anyone who adheres to the view that there is a difference between hard and soft often finds it difficult to fully justify this view when pressed.

A really good example of this can be found in some very recent research carried out by the Institute of Personnel and Development. The study concluded that a distinction can be made between the payback (short-term, hard measures) on training investment and the 'pay-forward' (longer-term, less tangible).

What they seem to fail to understand is that return on investment can only be looked at in hard terms. If development helps to bring about culture change (e.g. heightened customer awareness) a return may take longer to achieve but the return on investment for such development can still only be gauged in hard, added value terms (numbers of customers and customer spend). It would appear that not only is no progress being made on this subject, but the professional institute has managed to make a difficult subject even more complicated with this new, meaningless jargon.

The KPMT Added Value Model

In order to understand how the KPMT model – developed by the authors of this report – has been formulated a picture will be built up, initially using four levels of reaction – learning, behaviour/transfer and organisational added value – as a base.

First, we have to add one other level which comes in right at the beginning. We can call this 'base level'. This must be a clear business objective for which we already have a baseline, a bottom-line measure. So, we are looking to improve this measure, partly through a training and development intervention, and we will evaluate the training and development by remeasuring progress towards this objective after the training and development is completed.

In other words, we are going to see if the training and development added any value.

So, in short, the basic KPMT model is:

Base level –   Baseline business measures

Level 1   –   Reaction to the training and development

Level 2   –   Learning

Level 3   –   Transfer to the workplace/behaviour

Level 4   –   Bottom-line added value, measured in relation to the base level measures taken

Consequently the KPMT model is all about measuring added value.

We, therefore, define evaluation of training and development as **a measure of the value added by training and development**.

But what exactly do we mean by value? Figure 4.1 provides a very simple, but absolutely crucial, definition of added value.

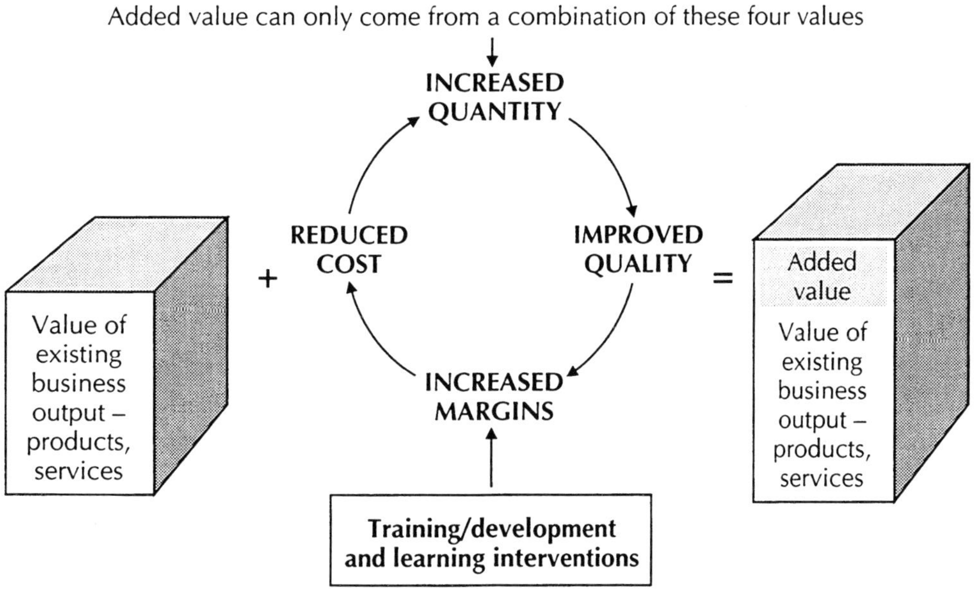

Added value can only come from a combination of these four values

Figure 4.1 Added value can always be measured in hard, bottom line terms.

The box on the left is meant to represent the value of your organisation. An accountant would be able to put a figure on this – even including a sum to cover goodwill.

The basic proposition for training and development is: will the box get bigger as a result of the training and development investment? If it does not, then the training and development cannot be said to be adding value and is, therefore, not worthwhile from the organisation's point of view.

Moreover, if you want to add value in any organisation, there are only a few key variables that you can influence which will result in added value. They are outputs, costs and prices (or margins). We can include 'improving quality' in the belief, hopefully, that improved quality will feed through to customer perceptions and result in more products or services being demanded, or commanding a higher price.

This obvious fact of life is often resisted by management development professionals because they do not like to see their work brought down to this hard, easily definable, lowest common denominator approach. But they cannot deny that it is true.

Also, none of these variables can be looked at in isolation. If costs go down, that will not automatically add value if the quality drops by a greater percentage. So added value is a holistic concept. If you get added value from something, you can rest assured that the complex web of variables in operation are coming together in a beneficial way.

This model can easily be seen as workable when applied to, say, production line operators. If training helps them to reduce costs while maintaining or even improving quality, then it can be seen to be adding value.

Now, if a model works for training production line operators, we can conclude that the fundamental principles underpinning the model are sound. So why shouldn't the same model be used to evaluate management development? It may be much more difficult to apply this simple model to what could be described as 'development activity', because such clear measures are not so readily available, but does that mean there is something intrinsically wrong with the model? Or, more alarmingly, does it mean that there is something inherently wrong with most conventional approaches to management development?

In fact, whoever said management development works? What about this quote from Dr Ian Cunningham, when he was still Chief Executive of the Roffey Park Management College in 1993:

> *Britain has been looking at the American business schools for the lead in management education for too long and copying approaches that simply don't work. Industrial performance in the US and UK has suffered consistently despite massive investment in management education that has largely proved inappropriate and ineffective.*

His recipe to improve matters was the notion of 'self-managed learning'. One could ask the question, hasn't learning always had to be self-managed?

So, the basic KPMT model appears to be sound for measuring training. We will come back to it later, to see how it can apply in the much more problematic areas of self-development and the learning organisation.

5 Placing evaluation in a national and international context. Or, why we have competencies and National Vocational Qualifications

It is important, at this stage, to place the need for the measurement and evaluation of training and development in a much broader context. This will not only emphasise its importance, but also indicate what other influences have come to bear on the subject, some of which are outside of the individual organisation's control. Consequently, no book on training and development, particularly evaluation, can be written today without acknowledging some of the large-scale, national initiatives.

No organisation can afford to regard itself as an island in the area of training and development. There are many factors, normally referred to as **externalities**, which come to bear. Take the construction industry as an example. Many construction companies employ people on short-term contracts and, therefore, may see no benefit in investing money in training and development. But if every construction company took this view, the whole industry would find itself without skilled tradesmen for the future. This was a prime reason why the Construction Industry Training Board survived when many other industry training Boards were disbanded.

Also, even though some organisations are excellent at training and development, they need to consider the fact that employees will want to carry with them, throughout their careers, evidence of the skills and knowledge they have obtained, in a form which is accepted by other organisations. Hence we see a reason for having a framework of nationally recognised qualifications.

National Vocational Qualifications (NVQs)

Studies into the subject of vocational qualifications and establishing a national framework date back to at least 1981 and the Manpower Service Commission's paper *An Agenda for Action.*

In very simple terms, if we look at what used to be a typical apprenticeship, there was always an element of 'time serving', that is, regardless of the skills and capabilities of the individual, they would not be deemed to be a craftsman until they had duly served an appropriate time in the trade – usually anything between four and seven years.

NVQs are based on the idea that jobs can be defined in terms of the standards required in the workplace, and that once someone can demonstrate that they can operate at this standard, they should be deemed as 'qualified'. In other words, if you can do the job why bother to look at the *length of time* in the job?

Moreover, if industry sectors set their own standards and are able to reliably assess performance against those standards, then there is a solid basis both for training, development and ultimately improvements in performance.

Unfortunately, the words 'reliably assess' gloss over what can be a very problematic process. It might be relatively easy to assess the standard for a bricklayer where the finished product is so apparent but what about service-related jobs and also supervisory or managerial roles?

NVQs are awarded on five different levels which equate, very approximately, to:

Level 1   –   Operator

Level 2   –   Craft

Level 3   –   Technician/supervisor

Level 4   –   Degree/professional/manager

Level 5   –   Senior manager

Defining standards at Levels 1 and 2 is not completely straightforward but at Level 3, and above, 'standards' of delegation, organisation and many of the other elements of a 'managerial' role become much more difficult to define and measure.

Because of this, in practice, NVQs have generated a great deal of jargon and can result in very time-consuming assessment activity such as collecting 'portfolios of evidence'. However, **if** NVQs really do get to the heart of what is required to perform effectively in a job, then they should be worthwhile but that 'if' becomes more and more critical from Level 3 up to Level 5.

Very closely allied to the idea of an NVQ framework is the theory of competence and the identification of competencies. In fact, NVQs would not exist without being underpinned by the belief that, for the job to be performed to the desired standard, all jobs can be broken down into a set of the competencies required.

Competencies

Never before in the world of training, education or development has one word been so widely debated, opinions so diverse and passions so aroused. The cause of all this consternation can be summed up in the one word – competencies. (Even the authors, normally sharing similar views on many other aspects of training and development, are in opposite camps when discussing the value and relative merits of adopting a competency framework.)

Needless to say, there is an enormous volume of literature on the subject and it is difficult to explore the potential impact of competencies on the bottom line in a short report. However, it is such an important subject because the whole theory of competencies provides the foundation for the current 'UK plc' training and development strategy (IIP and NVQs) which in turn underpin the competitive strategy promoted by the government. Consequently it has to be covered in sufficient depth here because the value of competencies is constantly coming under scrutiny.

What Are Competencies?

Broadly speaking, a competence is a combination of skills, knowledge, experience, personality traits and even attitudes and behaviour. Another way of describing them is to say they are the combination of what someone does, how they do it and what they have to know to do it in the workplace. Obviously, implicit in the definition of competence is the view that those individuals who possess it are able to perform better in their role than those who are not 'competent'.

Competencies are normally of a practical nature, usually associated with being able to do a task or activity in the workplace. The skills, knowledge and experience are normally grouped into a sensible complete task.

Take, for example, a supervisory qualification. A certificate in management practice, achieved through an exam from a college or by distance learning, could be said to be an acknowledgement that the individual has the requisite knowledge for a post involving a certain level of managerial content.

A competence or NVQ approach would require evidence that the individual can fulfil the requirements of the post to fixed standards, in practice, as well as having the correct amount of knowledge. *Doing* the job *properly* is critical to the concept of competence.

We could restate this by saying those who are competent can add greater value. If this is true then, in theory, the difference that competency development makes, that is the outcomes, should result in greater measurable outputs.

The application of *competencies* fall broadly into three categories: *job* competencies, *individual* competencies and *organisational* competencies. Getting the best added value from the use of a competency framework will not be achieved without getting to grips with the issue of where the true potential for added value lies in an organisation.

Individual competencies are developed throughout someone's life. These would normally include such competencies as writing skills, PC literacy, communication skills, etc.

Organisational competencies are those which the organisation sees as being necessary for its effective operation and where minimum standards have to be met. Take project management. The organisation may decide that certain of its management grades have to be fully competent in this area if a great deal of their work is structured around projects and running project teams.

The Management Charter Initiative (MCI) sees this sort of competence as critical for the competitive standing of 'UK plc' and are responsible for setting management standards in areas previously regarded as more a black art than a science.

Job competencies are relatively straightforward in that they are those which an individual must possess in order to fulfil the demands of their job.

Competency theory suggests that when such competencies are examined, there is a core group of competencies which are the key, critical factors in effective performance. Homing in on these competencies can, potentially, focus on the greatest potential area for enhancing added value though individual development.

One of the reasons why competencies appear so attractive as a developmental tool and framework is that, once identified, they can then be used for other purposes such as drafting job advertisements, interviewing and testing, and can even be linked into reward systems.

One alternative view on competencies is that the basic theory is flawed. For example, even if a range of competencies are identified for a particular managerial position, there are many questions that have to be asked, such as:

- If 'initiative' is described as a competence can an individual, currently without it, be developed to have initiative?

- Of all the competencies identified, do they all have different weightings in terms of how they influence performance? So does personal drive account for 50% of performance and delegation only 10%?

- Can people be developed 'jigsaw fashion'? If someone is developed in all of the relevant competencies, does that guarantee that they will perform? Or is the relationship between each of the competencies much more complex?

- What factors, outside of competencies, can significantly affect performance? The sort of things that immediately spring to mind are levels of authority and responsibility, organisation structure and reporting lines, business processes, personal motivation patterns. Can competencies succeed if these factors are not fully understood?

Regardless of the theory, how well do competencies seem to reflect reality? Think for a moment about managers in your own organisation. Focus on those regarded as the best performers. Do they all seem to share common traits, patterns of behaviour and levels of expertise? If they appear to have very little in common what does it suggest about using a competency approach to development?

Also, does their performance seem to change over time? In a very dynamic world, are the best managers of four or five years ago the best managers today?

There are many, many questions that should be posed before an organisation opts to install a comprehensive, competency-based, training and development system with a view to introducing NVQs.

The real relevance to this report, however, is that if competencies and NVQs are to make a measurable impact on the bottom line of your organisation, the fundamental first step of evaluation, 'what measurable effect do we want competencies and NVQs to have?', is still the only place to start.

Also, focusing on standards, which are not constantly linked to both individual and business performance, can result in more attention being paid to the number of NVQs achieved rather than the ultimate effect on the bottom line. To date, no clear and unequivocable evidence has been produced to show a direct link between competencies/NVQs and superior business performance.

Nevertheless, competencies and NVQs, despite being regarded in some quarters as another latest fad, are here to stay for the time being. Why is this so?

The 'UK plc' Position

Well, in 1987 the Training Agency, part of what was the Department of Employment, published a report entitled *Training in Britain* which highlighted a worrying gap between skills in the UK and those of its competitors (a state of affairs that seems to have remained resistant to significant improvement, it has to be said).

The UK, now, like all other western economies, is concerned about its competitive position in an ever-changing world where the pressures from relentless competition, particularly from the Pacific Rim and the Tiger economies, has started to train the spotlight on the state of our own corporate and economic strength and also the education and training infrastructure that underpin it.

Two respected academics on this subject, Dr Ewart Keep (Warwick Business School) and Ken Mayhew (Pembroke College, Oxford) provided an excellent summary of the arguments in their Scoping Paper for the *What Makes Training Pay* project, (IPD, 1994):

> *... A consensus has emerged that the British economy is faced with hard choices concerning the competitive strategies which can be adopted to meet the challenges of the 1990s and beyond. Many, such as the IPM (now IPD[1]), CBI[2], IoD[3], and the National Commission for Education, have argued that it is vital that we take steps towards a high skills, high productivity economy, where workers at all levels within firms, and across all sectors of the economy, become better qualified, more flexible, and self reliant in order to cope with the challenges of increased global competition, heightened product innovation, technological change, and post-Fordist product regimes wherein the customisation of goods and services will be the norm. Government guidance to the TECs[4] and LECs[5] refers to skills as the 'key to prosperity'.*

Whether such a strategy is likely to work is open to a great deal of debate which is set to continue to run for some time. But understanding that this strategic thinking lies behind government policy is important in the context of this book for several reasons.

- What *might* be true for the economy at a macro level does not necessarily mean that it holds true for every organisation at the

---

[1] Institute of Personnel and Development.

[2] Confederation of British Industry.

[3] Institute of Directors.

[4] Training and Enterprise Council.

[5] Local Enterprise Councils in Scotland.

micro level. Lifetime learning may not be at the top of the agenda for a business desperately trying to survive cut-throat competition.

- However, this strategy dominates national policy decisions and any organisation which wants to have its own training and development strategy will find it difficult to go down a different route to NVQs, for example, when so much effort and resources is being directed at national initiatives.

- If your organisation does not offer NVQs it may find it difficult to attract and retain some levels of staff. This may impose a pressure to offer NVQs but that then becomes a very different business reason for adopting a competency-based NVQ system. Staff retention may improve but does this automatically mean an improvement in your bottom line?

Perhaps the simple message is to be absolutely clear in your own mind why you choose to go down any particular route in training and development. Is it because that is the best option for your organisation in terms of performance, or is it because you are being pressurised to take a course of action which is not directly focused on business improvement? It is worth spending some time pondering this question before embarking on any costly and time-consuming training and development strategy.

The European Dimension

Very briefly, it is also worthwhile adopting a European perspective.

In 1994 the EU funded a project to produce 'A training model for European success' in small, medium and large organisations. The project concluded that there were five key areas for action and five key points on how the model might be achieved.

The 'What needs to be done' areas are:

- stimulation of creativity;

- continuous development;

- opportunities for all through empowerment;

- customer focus and involvement;

- international and cultural awareness.

The 'How to do it points' are:

- multiskilling and flexibility;

- business planning;

- communication;

- implementation and methodology;

- evaluation.

The need to link training to the business plan was an implicit, core element throughout the project.

One output from this project is a video currently being distributed by Dorset TEC[6].

Without going into too much detail, it is fully acknowledged throughout Europe that the ability to measure the effects of training and development on the bottom line is a major objective. So far, no single answer has been found to be acceptable.

William Tell and his Competencies

Finally, before we leave this section, consider the legend of William Tell and the apple on his son's head. If a trainer, who only understands validation and not evaluation, was asked to train William Tell for this task, what sort of steps might they adopt?

They could use the competency approach. This would involve analysing all the competencies required to be an expert with a crossbow. This might include adopting the right stance, perfect eyesight, knowing how to load and hold the crossbow correctly. Maybe they would even work on the perfect arm height or the angle at which William looked along the sight. Some more sophisticated trainers could even train William in how to judge wind speed and direction and the effect this might have on a crossbow bolt weighing so much.

They would then validate all of these competencies by observing William's behaviour and perhaps mathematically testing whether he had made the right adjustment for wind speed.

But would they ever measure whether the arrow hit the apple? Or, indeed, that at least it missed his son! Not unless they really understand that evaluation is about achieving the ultimate objective.

---

[6] Copies can be obtained by telephoning (01202) 299284.

6 The part evaluation plays in Investors in People

Having covered the broader issues in Chapter 5 we can understand why pressure from several business and professional organisations led to the conclusion that, to keep up with the best in the world, we had to make sure that training and development practices were keeping up. This thinking culminated in the launch of the Investors in People standard at the CBI conference in 1990.

In essence, it is meant to be a framework of good practice which is well thought out, practical and sets a nationally recognised standard covering four key areas, known as the four Principles of IIP:

- **Principle 1**: Public commitment from the top of the organisation to develop all employees.

- **Principle 2**: Regular reviews of the training and development needs of all its employees.

- **Principle 3**: An emphasis on action to train and develop employees from recruitment and right throughout their employment.

- **Principle 4: Evaluation of the business benefits from investment in training and development.**

Once achieved through a process of external assessment, organisations which have the standard are then reassessed on a three-yearly basis.

Perhaps one of the most explicit and unequivocal statements about the Investors in People view of training and development can be seen in the following statement, taken from a guide produced for Investors in People, Scotland, entitled *Evaluation of Training – Guidance for Managers*:

> The Investors in People approach treats the process of 'people development' in the same way as any other major business investment. It focuses people's activities and their training and development on the achievement of business goals and targets. It ensures that the investment in training and development provides 'value for money'.

If this is what IIP is really about, then it has to be able to evaluate that return on investment.

IIP as a Total Quality System

As a framework IIP is excellent. Although it does not explicitly state it in its literature, it is actually based on a typical, closed loop, total quality system. In practice, it starts from the business plan and the evaluation of the benefits is intended to act as a feedback loop to generate continuous improvements. It is a pity that 'evaluation' is Principle 4 though, because, as we have already seen, those who come to evaluation as an after-the-event requirement are going to be sorely disappointed.

The cycle in Figure 6.1 is based on the total quality cycle developed by the quality guru Deming. This is intended to be a systematic approach for continuous improvement.

Figure 6.1 A total quality cycle for training and development (T&D).

Total quality has to start with a plan to improve a business measure. Remeasuring provides a means of evaluating and reviewing whether the action is having the desired effect. The conclusions reached will either result in continuing in the same direction or mean that there has to be a revised plan. This is a never-ending, iterative process. The measures provide the means for a feedback loop to constantly check progress.

Effective evaluation is, therefore, one of the corner stones of the whole IIP framework. If this fails, the whole structure is undermined and can collapse. In total quality terminology, evaluation acts as a feedback loop. That is, it checks to see if what was planned actually happened. And yet, even though IIP has been in operation for five years, assessors of the standard have not been provided with a robust and reliable evaluation methodology. So they are unable to demonstrate achieving the standard has added value.

It is not surprising, therefore, to find that the Investors in People UK organisation, the main guardian of the standard, have made strenuous efforts to develop a workable, evaluation methodology. Unfortunately, at the time of writing, they have failed to produce such a methodology, although it appears that no one seeking accreditation under the standard is allowed an easy time when it comes to evaluation.

This is particularly worrying if one considers, then, how much of a real 'standard' exists when one of the cornerstones is liable to subside or shift at any time.

Despite this criticism, IIP is a worthwhile initiative and one that 'UK plc' has needed for a long time. Whoever devised Investors in People and designed the framework deserves a medal; but like all purveyors of good, but radical, new ideas, especially those which aim to get results, they would probably be pilloried for putting organisations through so much pain. But why should the IIP process be so painful for some and why has it not been taken up readily by many of the larger and, hopefully, more professional organisations, in training and development terms?

In Chapter 4, on evaluation models, the concept of total quality systems thinking based on feedback loops was used as the basis for the KPMT added value evaluation model. If you do not have a feedback loop in a training system, you have no way of knowing whether what you are doing is actually working.

Now let us consider, for a moment, the fact that most training and development over the years has been undertaken without any systematic or meaningful evaluation in place. This means, in practice, that no-one can say whether such training and development ever 'worked', because the loop was never closed and there would be no guarantee that the training was continuously improving.

So, without feedback loops the training and development activity could have been very poor and actually getting worse. That is, in a vicious circle or downward spiral. This is the opposite of a virtuous circle – the total quality cycle. This situation resulted in such deterioration in training design that we now have many organisations running menus of training courses without ever asking not only how good are they, but even worse – not bothering to ask whether there really is a need for such courses in the first place.

So, when IIP was launched and stated that those organisations seeking accreditation had to evaluate the business benefits of training, a national can of worms was, unsuspectingly, opened up. Evaluating training which has no clear objectives is not only impossible but even if you could measure any potential benefits, they are likely be very small indeed.

But if you are a training director or manager and have been responsible for running the function on this unfocused basis for many years, the last thing you want to do is admit that maybe much of your training was not delivering the goods. This is why changing attitudes to training and development has been so difficult and probably why IIP has made such limited in-roads into the large employer sector.

7 Evaluating existing training and development programmes

So far, we have tried to produce a template for installing training and development systems that will make an impact on the bottom line. By now, it should have become apparent to those who are already engaged in running significant numbers of training courses that the basic KPMT model in Chapter 4 is not designed to evaluate courses that did not have clear, measurable business objectives at the outset. And yet the authors fully appreciate that training and development practitioners come to their seminars and workshops, first and foremost, to find out how to evaluate *existing* programmes.

This raises a very sensitive subject and one that will not be side-stepped. If a training course has been running for several years as part of a training department's menu or catalogue of courses, and no evaluation measures were built in, then it is possible, in theory, that such a course has added no value to the organisation whatsoever. Unfortunately, though, without any evaluation measures in place, no one would be able offer irrefutable proof one way or the other.

This places the training practitioner in a very awkward position. The dilemma is: 'Do I now try to evaluate something that may not have any value or do I forget trying to evaluate my existing courses and start to design new courses, programmes and interventions with evaluation built-in?'

This chapter is a constructive and positive attempt to help those who find themselves in this predicament.

Basic Versus Added Value Training and Development

One way forward is to start from our earlier distinction between **basic** (or minimum requirement) training and **added value** training and development.

Basic training was defined as ensuring a level below which the organisation cannot fall if it wishes to remain operating effectively. If the organisation can exist without it, then it is not a minimum requirement. So, for example, a minimal requirement for a bank clerk to be able to deal with customers on their own might be an ability to undertake credit and debit transactions. The ability to sell the bank's insurance services at the same time might be regarded as requiring added value training and development.

Why is it worth looking at training and development from this perspective? The main reason is highlighted by Figure 7.1 and putting this into practice is covered in Appendix 1, Tool Number 4.

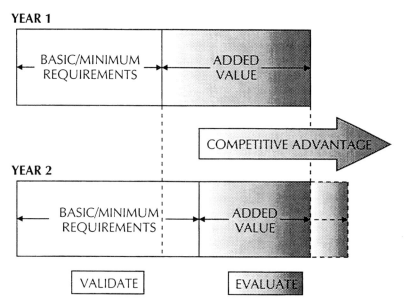

Figure 7.1 Basic and added value training and development.

Once the basic/added value split is completed, it can be stated quite clearly that the training in the basic box must be achieved for the well-being of the business.

In effect, this is stating that this type of training is absolutely crucial and mandatory. Therefore, its real value to the business is taken as read and no actual measurement of value is necessary.

On the other hand, anything that falls into the added value box is discretionary. The business will survive without it for the time being, but if this training and development activity is carried out effectively, it will bring extra benefits with it. It could even be regarded as the competitive advantage box.

However, while the basic box does not require detailed evaluation measures because its value is self-evident, the discretionary, added value box must be evaluated. This is because questions concerning how much benefit it can bring, and the corresponding cost, must be asked if this training and development activity is to be embarked upon. Investment in this area will also have to compete for funds with other projects in the business so a return on investment case has to be created.

But the first priority, for those who have never done evaluation before, is to ensure, at the very least, that the basic training is covering all the minimum requirements and is being delivered effectively.

Why Validation Is Also Important

Basic training only needs to be validated because its value is guaranteed by the fact that the organisation must have it. Now we can see why validation is still important. Existing basic training should be validated using Steps 1, 2 and 3 of the KPMT model. If the validation measures show that there is a deficiency in this type of training then it can be seen as having a direct, negative effect on the business. If learning how to answer the telephone properly is part of basic training, then a simple sampling of how calls are answered will immediately say if customer service is suffering and whether something needs to be done about it.

This report is not concerned, primarily, with validation techniques, partly because validation is generally less important than evaluation, but also because there is plenty of literature, readily available, on different tools and techniques for validation (even though it is normally referred to as evaluation!).

Added Value Becomes a Basic Requirement in the Long Term

But that is not the end of the story. Figure 7.1 also tries to illustrate how, in the real world of relentless competition, what might add value today is likely to become the basic training of tomorrow. The basic and added value blocks are likely to constantly move. If a higher level of basic training is required (now having to teach the bank clerk about insurance policies to keep up with the competition) then the cost of basic training is bound to increase. The main business issue here, therefore, is to be able to deliver more and more basic level training to the required standard at the least cost.

Meanwhile, the added value box is being squeezed and the benefits reduced because all your competitors are doing the same and it brings no added value or competitive edge benefits. Consequently, more and more ideas have to be generated to push the added value sector out further (the cashier now tries to prompt enquiries about pensions).

This movement can easily be seen to be happening in virtually any mature or fiercely competitive business sector.

So, when the existing, basic training is fully validated the training practitioner can turn their attention to the more interesting area of added value.

Applying Nominal Evaluation Measures

It might be tempting to 'validate' the added value box first but it is important not to forget that the value of this training has not been guaranteed yet – it was discretionary.

Without having built-in evaluation, of course, it is *impossible* to evaluate training that is already taking place – but you have to start somewhere. The object of this exercise is not so much to put a real, bottom line value on the training and development but to try and sort out which training and development events make a difference in performance and which do not.

To do this requires making some assumptions. At one of the author's seminars, one of the audience, a trainer from a high street bank, suggested that he would welcome any assistance in evaluating an assertiveness training course which had been running for years with a total of at least 1500 participants having been put through the course.

Where would we start to evaluate this? Needless to say there were no clear business improvement areas targeted when the course was designed. So we have to look at the 'implicit theory' behind running such a course.

No doubt this theory would go something like this. If we send a manager on this course, who has been recognised as lacking in assertiveness, then when they return to work they will start to be more assertive in their dealings with, say, customers. Perhaps if they are negotiating loans, then they may improve their bad debt ratio by dealing with poor payers more assertively, showing them they mean business and maybe even threatening them with stronger action than they would have done in the past.

We can already see how this particular theory would have to be adapted to each individual participant's set of circumstances for it to stand a chance of working in practice. But let us not get too pernickety.

If this is the theory behind the training, then to apply evaluation techniques the trainer would have to look at bad debt ratios of all the managers who had been on the course over the last ten years. But let us be absolutely clear about the problems this 'reverse engineering' approach has.

- Which implicit theory do you want to work to? Would different theories be needed for all the different types of staff put through the course?

- What if the figures showed that the improvements predicted by the theory had not been achieved?

- Even if there was an improvement, would anyone believe that there was a link between this training course and the improvement?

- How many other variables would be cited to question any correlation between this particular course and business improvement?

It is not an exercise that is likely to achieve anything worthwhile and it is unlikely that the trainer would be able to collect the necessary data without a great deal of hard work.

At another seminar, a lady who worked for a building society could not accept that it is impossible to evaluate existing training which is not focused on the bottom line.

To make this point absolutely clear the seminar participants were split into two groups. The training to be evaluated was the building society's coaching skills module for supervisors.

One group tried to evaluate this training module, and the other used the simple KPMT model to see if coaching skills could be focused on measurable operational improvements in a public utility organisation.

Figure 7.2 shows how this exercise turned out and tries to make a distinction between what could be called **focused** and **unfocused** training and development.

The problem with evaluating unfocused training is that at some stage in the process you have to define what you mean by 'better' or 'improvement' and these terms, by definition, mean that measures have to be attached. This brings us back to the question of which measures to use, and the only measures we are interested in are bottom line, added value, business performance measures.

So let us look at how such measures can be built in for evaluation purposes.

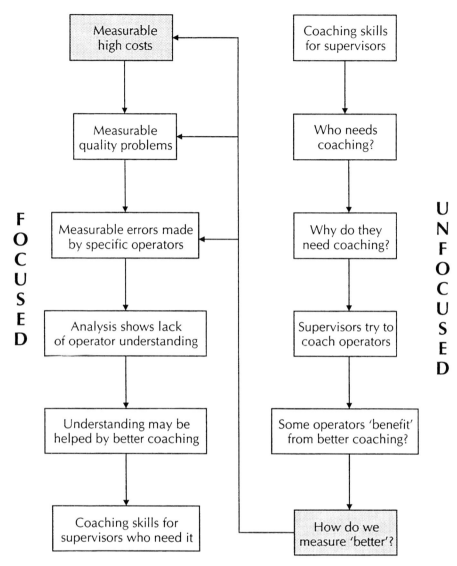

Figure 7.2 Evaluating focused and unfocused training and development.

Part Two

An Advanced Level
Approach to Evaluation

8 Building evaluation into training and development

How much benefit you have obtained from this report so far will depend, to a greater or lesser extent, on where you are already in evaluation terms. The basic version of the KPMT model covered in Chapter 4 will have enabled you to start to look at evaluation in bottom-line terms.

Anyone who has already spent some time evaluating training, though, will have realised that evaluation is only straightforward when there are obvious opportunities for business improvement through straightforward training interventions. Reducing production costs through quality training to reduce scrap rates is a good example.

Often, the real success stories heard from Investors in People and the National Training Awards (NTA) are from organisations where significant or step improvements are still possible, and achievable, through training and development initiatives.

It is highly questionable, however, whether they are good examples of evaluation best practice. Research carried out by Saville and Holdsworth into 35 NTA winners from 1992 found that although 60% of these supposedly 'evaluated' (sic) all their training events, 75% of that 'evaluation' consisted of only the end-of-course happy sheet. In our terminology, this means that only approximately 15% of 'evaluation' in this total group, of nationally recognised award winners, ever got past the very simple first level of validation.

Even if the evaluation measures showed good results, such step improvements become harder and harder to find in an organisation that has been practising the philosophy of continuous improvement for some years. Here, the potential benefits from training and development are not so obvious and the ability to pick training and development needs out of a complex set of variables requires higher level skills.

To use the same principles in a more complex environment now requires a modified and more advanced version of the basic KPMT model. The starting point is still the question 'what measurable effect do we want training and development to have on the business?' and the last step is the same, remeasuring any difference achieved, but two other steps have to be included.

The KPMT Added Value Model in Practice

At the insurancy company Frizzell, a six-step model has been in operation for some years.

Step 1: Discuss the Needs of the Business

In order to start with business objectives and focused training and development, business-related training and development requirements are discussed with the managers concerned.

This discussion will normally be based on the business plans that the managers are working to and should take place during the business planning process, if possible.

But this is not a case of just asking managers 'what training and development can I do for you?'! This should be a discussion which looks at the business needs and any pressure points or likely areas of performance deficiencies which can be addressed through training and development.

It is quite possible that there are no obvious areas in which training and development can help, and even if the managers suggest that there are, the customer is not always right.

The dialogue might centre on a need for a 10% improvement in sales performance. First, the business plan should spell out whether this is in terms of sales volumes, price increases or new product introductions. Each one would indicate different possible training and development support.

If it was a straight 10% increase in existing volumes, the next obvious question would be 'how do you intend to achieve this increase?'. Half the increase might be expected to come from raising the number of sales visits and growing the customer base. The other half could be based on an average improvement of 5% in each salesperson's performance.

So, is training required in:

- visit scheduling?

- opening new accounts?

- cold calling?

- individual performance monitoring?

- coaching skills for the manager?

This is the sort of discussion that has to take place, but the key is to start indicating the size of the improvement required from the training and development input – in this case, up to half of the overall 10% increase. What exactly is that in £s and is it to be spread evenly across all sales regions?

Step 2: Design Some Proposed Training and Development Solutions

Based on the initial discussion at Step 1, the training and development 'analyst' can start to put together a range of training and development initiatives to help deliver the business improvement required, and separate out any areas that are not likely to be affected by training and development.

Step 3: Decide on the Real Training Issues and Agree a Contract

This is an iterative step. Initial ideas about how training and development can help are fed back to the internal customer with clearly defined outputs so that a contract can be agreed for training to deliver what is required.

This is a crucial step in ensuring commitment and buy-in from line managers.

Step 4: Deliver

How the training and development is delivered is a big question with a multitude of options. Here, someone with expertise to choose the appropriate cost-effective solution is very important.

Step 5: Evaluate

This is a relatively easy step in this model because the measures to be used for evaluation purposes are those already part of the contract at Step 3 – unlike in most other evaluation models where the actual evaluation measurement can be very time consuming.

Step 6: Feedback

This step is not just about publicising results but giving honest feedback (as in a total quality system) to everyone involved in this particular training contract. It is not just about giving good news either. If things did not work out as planned, then this should result in a thorough review and everyone should learn from their experiences.

It is also worth noting that although Tony Miller, one of the authors of this report, adheres to the principle of continuous improvement, he is always prepared to move on to other areas when a particular training and development initiative has achieved its original business objectives.

Have you noticed, though, that the first step demands most of the attention? If you get this right, everything falls into place. If you get it wrong, the training and development is never likely to be very successful. This is the most crucial area of skills development for anyone whose function is to analyse business-related training and development needs, in order to design and deliver training and development with built-in evaluation.

Using Bottom-Line Measurement in Training Needs Identification and Analysis

A UK training and development manager for an engineering company asked one of the authors for help on evaluation. Within minutes of the conversation starting, the basic principles of the KPMT model were laid before him. His immediate reaction was that this approach seemed to be very time consuming and what he really wanted was some quick and easy way to improve on their existing 'evaluation' measures (which only amounted to happy sheets and some minimal course follow-up).

He was asked how training and development needs were currently identified and he replied that a 'Step 1' discussion, much like that illustrated in the KPMT model above, took place with managers when they had their business plans for the following year.

When he was advised that this was the time to start building in evaluation by asking managers what business improvement they wanted from training and development, he said that neither his training staff nor the line managers would have either the time or the inclination to go into the depth suggested by the KPMT model.

This was, more or less, where the meeting came to an end. The training manager was still not convinced that this was the only way to start true evaluation.

Regardless of all the issues raised by this one short scenario, which is probably representative of many attitudes to evaluation, probably the most damning point is that people do not seem to understand that 'not having the time' is no excuse for designing unfocused training and development. If training is an investment with an expected business return, then the amount of time allowed for this Step 1 discussion will be dictated by the size of potential business benefit expected.

Similarly, if there are no significant improvement areas identified, then why not forget about doing any training and development at all?

The message from this is twofold:

- making enough effort, at the initial analysis stage, to get a bottom line measure to start from is usually worth it in the long run because it will ensure that value-less training stops and high added value training starts off on the right foot;

- the reason line managers often think it is not worth their time is because they do not attach any real value to training and development. They pay lip service to it and will use it for every reason except the achievement of bottom-line objectives.

To get over all the hurdles associated with these outmoded traditional perceptions of training and development and to re-educate managers (including training managers) requires developing good questioning techniques – as well as being prepared to be very assertive and honest when managers try to fob you off with bad answers or pressure you to deliver quick fixes or management entertainment courses.

Both authors are in 100% agreement when it comes to this point. If a business objective cannot be cited as a basis for designing training and development then no training and development should be offered.

So, having a meaningful discussion which searches for bottom-line improvements from training and development has to be the starting point, even if, in the early days of changing perceptions, this requires consummate tact and diplomacy.

Once the discussion starts to focus on the bottom-line, progress can be made.

Evaluation as an Aid to Training Design

So this initial discussion will end with a statement such as 'if we do that type of training and development it is intended to deliver this business improvement'.

But will you ever get to that point? The KPMT added value model starts to really come into its own, surprisingly enough, at the design stage because the metrics used will indicate how much to spend and the best way to spend or target it.

If an engineering director wants his sales engineers to be trained in presentation skills then there are many courses around which would apparently satisfy his, and their, requirements quite easily. Or would they?

If the initial discussion started to look at the engineering director's own business objectives set by the managing director, there may be one which involves his staff making successful business presentations to clients as part of a team. This could be a very valid business objective but is any measurement attached to it? If no one is measuring the success of these presentations then no one will be able to evaluate the training carried out to support it.

Simple measurement questions about how many presentations take place and how often engineers are involved will start to look at possible training needs. Then, digging a little deeper – 'how many of these engineers are not presenting satisfactorily at the moment?' – will avoid wasting money on those who are already competent presenters (did anyone in the bank ask these simple questions before sending people on assertiveness courses?). Interestingly enough, it will also avoid demotivating those who already regard themselves as proficient at presentations.

Once the key people have been identified, it would then be necessary to ask the difficult evaluation questions. Perhaps start with 'how many presentations last year were really badly influenced by poor presentation skills?', 'did we lose any important contracts following these presentations or what other effects did this have?'

Here, we are getting closer to seeking out the bottom-line measures. Let us assume that one presentation went particularly badly and it was on a large contract tender that was lost to a competitor. Perhaps the managing director had a fit and decreed that presentations had to be improved immediately (you might sense that this is actually based on a real example).

If this is where the questioning led then it starts to become apparent that it probably is not just a case of poor presentation skills by engineers. Who organised that presentation and coordinated it? Was the engineer in question well briefed?

If we stop here and now look at training needs it could be that the main training requirement is not the actual presentation skills but minimum standards for all engineers to follow before they are put in front of potential customers. Perhaps the real problem is guaranteeing that, at every presentation in future, engineers will check their briefing fully with the team leader first and then deliver a presentation to an agreed format which fits with everyone else on the team.

And how would such training be evaluated? Well, perhaps it is actually basic training after all and the best measure is validation, simply to ensure that this standard is reached at every future presentation.

So, in effect, we are using bottom-line evaluation questions as part, not only of the training needs analysis phase, but also the training design phase. The answers to these searching questions will help to point to the best training method to be used. In this case it might be a short session on pre-presentation planning, not just a typical presentation skills course.

Evaluation as a Means of Ensuring Management Commitment

The other major issue here is the level of commitment from the engineering director to any training that might subsequently be delivered. Anyone who has had responsibility for managing a training department will know, from bitter experience, that getting management commitment and buy-in is one of the biggest hurdles that has to be overcome. There are many reasons for this, such as the time involved, getting them interested in something outside of their normal operation and so on.

In simple terms, the main reason why it has been difficult to get this commitment in the past is because if evaluation models have been weak then the management concerned would not have been asked, up front, what business improvements they want from their training effort. Hence they are asked to commit to something not directly focused on helping them achieve their own business objectives.

Therefore, the added value model aims to build this level of commitment in right from the start. In fact, if a clear business objective is not identified and measured in advance then why not take a hard line and say that no training will take place until these preconditions have been met?

One training manager, in an electronic components company, agreed with the sales director to design a training programme for the sales team. After three months of hard work she proudly presented the new course programme to the sales director only to be told that the training was no longer a priority!

If the engineering director in the earlier example above is not prepared to have an in-depth discussion on the real training needs, then his commitment is likely to be minimal and he may only be doing something to keep the managing director happy. This is the real world, but if you work in training and development do you want to make a difference or deliver political expediency? The value of the latter, in bottom-line terms, is probably nil and any benefits for personal survival are likely to be very short-lived because personal credibility will not be achieved from badly designed training.

For trainers, being assertive at this stage in this process and having the requisite skills to turn vague ideas about training into clear business objectives will pay great dividends – not only to the business but in terms of job satisfaction as well.

For directors and managers who believe training and development will help them achieve business objectives, be prepared for some lengthy discussions – but the rewards will come later. This is advanced quality planning applied to training and development – and about time too!

9 Empowerment, self-development and the learning organisation

So far this report has tried to steer a straight course through all the latest fads and fashions in management thinking. Jargon and buzzwords abound in the field of training and development and it is sometimes difficult not to be sucked in by their seductive tones. Those who have the audacity to question whether they make any difference to organisation performance risk being seen as negative.

Often there is a tendency to be either 'for' or 'against' a particular fashion. But, in reality, it is not as simple as just taking sides. Take something like business process re-engineering (BPR) – is it a good thing to be doing or not? Well, maybe that is the wrong question. Does a particular organisation, at a particular time, have a set of circumstances which is causing it serious problems that can best be addressed by a total and thorough review of its core business processes? If so, then maybe BPR is a possible answer and, if you are lucky, it may be the best option available.

There is nothing wrong with the methodology of BPR *per se*, or any other tool or technique for that matter. We do not seem to have progressed very far from the old adage that a poor craftsman blames his tools. Exactly the same accusation could be fired at numerous consultants and business leaders who embark on sophisticated change programmes without knowing exactly how the tools work and then blaming the tools when the hoped-for benefits of the programme fail to materialise.

Management tools, techniques, methodologies and even philosophies are often seen as universal panacea even though they are particularly difficult to use successfully in practice. How often are BPR programmes, TQM programmes or even culture change programmes instigated in the vain hope that they are going to bring with them numerous benefits? Such initiatives can bring substantial benefits and create a genuine competitive advantage but they have to be fully understood if the potential rewards are to be realised.

In an excellent article on this subject entitled 'Successful change programmes begin with results' (by Robert H. Schaffer and Harvey A. Thomson, *Harvard Business Review*, January–February 1992) it is argued that many change programmes fail because they become focused on activities rather than results. The authors conclude that:

> The performance improvement efforts of many companies have as much impact on operational and financial results as a ceremonial rain

dance has on the weather.... This 'rain dance' is the ardent pursuit of activities that sound good, look good and allow managers to feel good – but in fact contribute little or nothing to bottom line performance.

In training and development, some of the most commonly quoted buzzwords are the notions of empowerment, self-development and the search for something called the learning organisation. For those who believe work should be fulfilling for the individual and allow for personal growth these are wonderfully attractive concepts.

But do they also fit with those, like the authors, who always look, first and foremost for the bottom-line results? In a word, yes.

Notions such as self-development, often seen as a soft area, and bottom-line results are not mutually exclusive objectives. In fact, in a mature organisation they may well be totally mutually inclusive and commercially imperative.

The basic problem is that some of these concepts are taken out of context and applied in organisations that are not ready for them. So let us try to link some of these concepts coherently and in a chronological, evolutionary sequence.

If we look at a manufacturing organisation which decides that it has to improve its products or the level of service it offers, it has to start from a position where it knows how badly it is performing and where the problem areas are. From a quality point of view, it has to measure the quality of its product and install some form of **quality control**. So it may immediately put quality control inspectors at the end of the production line who find that 20% of its finished products have to be scrapped or reworked.

Only when it understands the size and nature of the problems it is facing can it start to do something about them. However, it will soon become apparent that having inspectors at the end of the line does nothing to stop problems that may occur in the first stages of the production process. So the idea of **quality assurance** is born: building quality in at every stage of the process.

Once it has dealt with all the obvious problems it begins to find it more difficult to find ways to improve quality or reduce costs further. What it finds is that supervisors, quality assurance staff and managers are not skilled enough at analysing the causes of potential quality problems and therefore have no basis for solving them.

Here the problem-solving tools and techniques normally associated with **TQM** programmes (Pareto, cause and effect, failure analysis, etc.) come into play and these people have to be trained to use these techniques.

Following a further evolutionary stage in the development of the company (by now probably several years down this road), it begins to dawn on all the managers that they cannot 'manage in' quality all the time when they are at the mercy of the skills, capabilities and attitudes of operators on the production line. So to achieve even further improvement the operators themselves have to become more involved in the quality assurance process and **empowered** to put things right.

They are even less able to use the problem-solving tools and techniques without some formal training and there may even be gaps in their basic education standards (do they know how to produce a simple histogram? Here we start to move into the very sensitive world of reassessing our whole education system). So great effort goes into training and developing operators, except that some of them, being on the bottom rung of the organisation and having never been asked for an input before, are totally disenchanted with the company and see no reason why they should adopt a different attitude. Consequently, we see moves towards developing new relationships between employer and employee along the lines of a **new psychological contract**.

Part of the drive to make workers more flexible and able to resolve problems as they arise requires a level of development in each individual which is difficult to identify for everyone. Hence there is a move more towards **self-development**, often supported by company learning centres where employees can find out all they need to know on a wide range of topics. As this particular aspect of the total quality revolution evolves, the lines between working, training and learning become blurred and we have the beginnings of something equating to a **learning organisation**.

Almost simultaneously, the benefits of rigid hierarchical organisation structures come under scrutiny, when operators require less and less supervision and are empowered to make their own decisions. Also, when the company has improved things as much as it can with its existing operational set up, it starts to seek even greater improvements by reassessing the business processes used in the organisation to see if they can be streamlined or made more effective; hence the drive towards **business process re-engineering**.

This simple illustration is meant to show that some of the terms we regard as fads are all logical, sequential steps arising out of an inexorable drive for continuous improvement. What is more, all of these initiatives should be installed to achieve **measurable, bottom-line improvements**. They should not be embarked on just because they are the latest fad.

A more subtle, but equally crucial point is that if the sequence of these developments is wrong, then the realisation of any potential benefits will be severely restricted. For example, how many organisations have attempted a fundamental BPR programme without having supported its employees through a process of self-development and empowerment? And yet without these preconditions the real benefits of BPR, which come from giving people new roles in more effective processes, are unlikely to be realised. It is interesting that much of the criticism currently directed at BPR initiatives centres around their failure to fully understand the people implications of redesigning core processes.

Although the following list may not be 100% accurate, it gives a brief overview of the sort of sequence that has taken place in organisations that get the total quality, continuous improvement philosophy right in practice:

- Quality control

- Quality assurance

- TQM

- Empowerment

- Self-development

- Business process re-engineering

- The learning organisation

- The new psychological contract

Moving Towards Lifelong Learning

If the above sequence does hold true for the economy generally, what we are in the middle of is a highly dynamic situation where everything is changing so rapidly that traditional approaches to training and development just cannot keep pace. The skills and knowledge base of the workforce can become obsolete very quickly. This is fully recognised by the government's national training strategy and their answer is to promote notions of lifelong learning and employability – where the individual accepts responsibility for their own, ever-changing learning needs in order to remain employable.

Both of these concepts have a nice ring to them but to what extent are they workable in practice? Suffice it to say that there are never going to be jobs for life again and those who think they only have to learn a single trade or profession are very quickly going to find themselves surplus to requirements.

In terms of evaluation, though, the links between all of these concepts and business performance should be made explicit at every possible opportunity. They should all make commercial sense, but saying that and meaning it can often be quite different things. These concepts, and where they fit, has to be fully understood by those formulating the high-level strategies for the organisation.

10 Strategic measurement of training and development

What is Strategic Training and Development?

Although the idea of taking a strategic approach to training and development has been touched on throughout this report, virtually all of the training and development examples given have been based on operational needs.

But eventually, as suggested earlier, all the obvious improvement areas and easy targets will be dealt with and the room for further improvement becomes more difficult. As a result, the significant opportunities for training and development become less obvious.

However, the search for step improvements is always too tempting to be called off, even though the only areas left for such gains are to be found by fundamentally rethinking the way you do business. For example, if excellent customer service is the only way left to differentiate your company from its competitors then the ability to engender the right attitudes, behaviour, motivation, freedom to act and individual capabilities of your employees at all levels, *and harness them*, becomes the only way to stay ahead. Unfortunately, to achieve this position is certainly *not* just a simple case of increasing the number of your customer service training courses.

Some organisations think that to achieve such ends is just a case of doing more, but maybe different, training and development. They do not understand that such change usually requires a fundamental shift in organisational thinking and culture. Others realise that a culture shift will be required but seem to regard that as just a matter of cultural re-training courses. Some even have 'change management programmes', probably one of the worst ways to bring about lasting change! Change, for most people, is a frightening and unsettling time. Just mention the word change and they will want to hide back inside their shells.

What very few organisations seem to understand is that such cultural shifts are inevitably going to take a considerable amount of time (and we are probably talking years), effort and commitment. Moreover, it requires someone at the top to have a vision of how things might be in the future in terms of organisation and operating practices. Alternatively, if it is decided that the organisation does not have time to spare, other radical options might need to be deployed. One could think of Times Newspapers moving into Wapping as a good example of a decision to make a fundamental and complete break with the past.

Many organisations would not dream of taking such a radical decision so they try to bring about change gradually. To have a chance of succeeding at this requires nothing short of a long-term, strategic view, and training and development may have a significant part to play. But where does strategic thinking in relation to training and development have to start?

Well, where else can it start, other than at the business strategy formation stage? If it starts any later than this there is a good chance the training and development strategy will not be integrated with the business strategy and will become a detached, reactive activity – without ownership by the board, or the line managers who will have to be instrumental in making it happen in practice.

Figure 10.1 shows how various levels of thinking in strategy formulation can fit, not only with training and development, but more importantly with the critical areas of organisation structure development and process design.

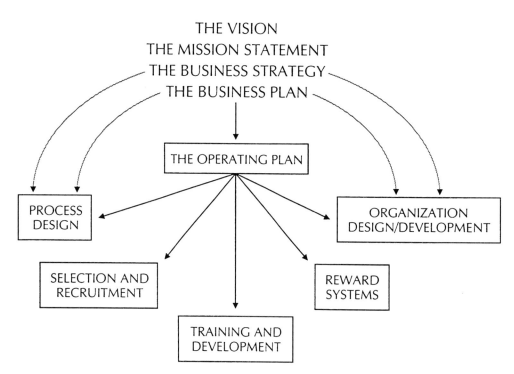

Figure 10.1 Where does training and development fit with business strategy?

The two biggest hurdles to overcome when trying to make training and development strategic are:

•   totally re-educating board members and line managers about where training and development can contribute strategically; and

- having strategic training and development tools, techniques and skills at your disposal so that you can deliver strategic, bottom-line improvements from training and development.

As part of the re-education process, perhaps a good starting point is to move away from training and development as a cost and move towards a model of training and development as an investment – and one which should be subject to all the considerations and controls that any other financial investment would normally attract.

Use this calculation when justifying training costs:

% Return on Investment (ROI) =

$$\frac{\text{Benefits from training (£s)} - \text{Costs of training (£s)}}{\text{Costs of training (£s)}}$$

If training costs are not perceived to be a genuine investment, just like any other corporate investment, then they will be treated as a 'pure' cost, that is a cost with no corresponding return or benefit, and as such there will always be undue pressure to reduce that cost. Similarly, referring to 'costs' all the time, without always considering the expected return on that cost, will only ever draw attention to one side of the coin, that is training at minimum cost, rather than focusing on value for money and return on investment.

From a strictly accounting point of view, strenuous efforts should be made to avoid having training expenditure classified as part of overheads. Overheads are always discussed at board meetings in the same tones as a nasty disease which has to be eradicated.

Furthermore, some organisations may well believe that training and development can help to fulfil a vision or mission statement, but these do not normally have any clear measures attached to them and so the links between training and development and strategic success are often tenuous at best. So, 'being first choice for our customers' and doing customer service training is a very simplistic approach to linking training and development to business strategy.

Training and development has to be linked to something tangible. If a mission statement says 'We want to be the first choice for customers in the high street' it does not provide the training and development function with a clear objective to link their activity to.

Questions such as 'How many more customers do we have to attract to be "first choice"?' and 'What does their average spend have to be to satisfy our business plans?' start to translate broad, and sometimes nebulous, strategic thinking into something more specific and tangible. Only by going through such a process can a training and development plan begin to have a clear focus and produce costings which can be justified in terms of expected business returns.

Significant progress will never be made, though, while training budgets are produced in the disconnected, *ad hoc* way that many of them are. If this sounds a little harsh, consider the high street bank which, when it came to a fundamental overhead review, did not even know how much it was spending on training, never mind having a sound, commercial basis for such a significant cost. Needless to say, the subsequent cuts were made on a completely arbitrary basis.

To achieve a genuine perception of training costs as a business investment requires using all the business justification tools available. The key message is to ensure that there is a common, agreed view of exactly where training expenditure fits. This will not only avoid confusion and arguments later on but will also dictate who controls the budget and who has authority to change it.

This leads us to the most advanced, strategic version of the KPMT evaluation model.

Advanced Methods in Evaluation

Perhaps one additional reason why there has been little progress in evaluation in practice which has not been mentioned so far is the difficulty of attributability. That is, even if we have clear, measurable business objectives before we start to design a training and development initiative, and the results show an improvement, how can we be sure that the results are due entirely to the training and development? It is often used as an excuse to avoid doing any evaluation at all.

But is it a valid question? It is usually of concern to those training and development professionals who have not clearly demonstrated that they add value through their efforts. But is anyone else interested in the matter?

Boards of directors are only really interested in achieving their strategic goals. They may well look to areas of the business that are not pulling their weight or blocking progress but generally they do not spend a great deal of time trying to apportion contributions.

Also, even if sales or production targets are achieved, does anyone say that their achievement was solely down to the sales and production functions? Of course not.

So attributability can be either a bit of a red herring or a smoke screen depending on your own choice of metaphors.

The reason that it is raised here as an issue, is that when we are looking at strategic decisions and the strategic direction of organisations, there are so many complex variables which come into play. We could get totally bogged down in trying to unravel them and isolate exactly which ones are to be influenced by training and development.

We have already established, though, that the answer is not to jump straight into training solutions from some vague mission statement without any clear links or measurements attached.

Instead, we have modified the basic version of the KPMT model to ensure that it addresses the issue of complexity but in such a way that it will lead to action rather than paralysis.

Table 10.1 provides the full, modified version which still contains the basic five levels in Chapter 4 but injects four other steps.

Table 10.1 The advanced, 9-step KPMT added value evaluation model

Step 1	What business output measures are you trying to improve?
Step 2	Who has an impact on those outputs, how and by how much?
Step 3	Can their impact be improved through HRD interventions?
Step 4	What bottom-line 'tell-tales' can be used to measure small improvements?
Step 5	What learning or training/development objectives can deliver the required improvements?
Step 6	How are the participants reacting to the HRD input?
Step 7	Are they learning what they are meant to learn?
Step 8	Are they using the learning at work?
Step 9	Has the intervention had the desired effect on the business output measures?

The basic KPMT model is covered by Steps 1, 6, 7, 8 and 9 but there are another four steps (2, 3, 4 and 5) included.

The question posed at Step 2 may look innocuous enough but it is intended to open up the whole question of whether the organisation has the most appropriate organisation structure and most effective and efficient processes that it needs to maximise value creation.

Let us apply this question to a company wishing to increase its market share by 5%. Developing the company's marketing managers in an unfocused way as part of this aim would be much too simplistic and have every chance of failing.

Can a marketing manager influence market share purely through their own activities? Look at the other influences that have to be taken into account:

- Are they allowed to dictate their own marketing spend?

- What say do they have in product development?

- Even if they have the right products for the right market, can their production people produce the goods at the right price and quality?

- Who else is involved in the broader question of marketing? Sales staff, public relations, technical staff? How much effect will other staff have on marketing?

This list could be very long and extremely complex. So do you just become paralysed by the enormity of it, saying life is too complicated? Or do you try to produce the best training and development plan you can, which addresses as many of these influences as possible?

One way to start to deal with this complexity is to start viewing your organisation as a series of interlinked process chains where each individual's contribution can be identified for improvement purposes.

Added Value Process Chains

There are some key points about processes that anyone involved in training and development must understand:

- a process turns inputs into outputs;

- value is added through processes;

- if a process does not add value it is not a business process;

- value can only be added to products, services and outputs;

- people need effective processes to perform effectively;

- people need efficient processes to perform efficiently;

- training and development cannot increase added value if it does not know how value is added.

Perhaps the last item on this list is the most telling point of all.

Look at Tool Number 5 to get an idea of how to use process thinking and process mapping in a training and development context.

Providing some of the answers to the questions at Step 2 is not the end of the story, though. Step 3 then checks whether any improvement targets identified can be achieved through training and development as opposed to other means such as organisation or process redesign.

If there is an opportunity for training and development to have an impact and some size is put on this impact, some measurement system needs to be put in place to check improvement trends. Normally this will mean graphing incremental sales, cost or quality changes over a period of time.

Then, after all this effort, there is still the need to translate the identified business improvement needs into specific training and development or learning objectives. This in itself requires a very highly developed skill set.

Only when all this has been done can the learning take place and the normal validation and evaluation measures start (Steps 6–9).

The New Role for Training and Development Professionals

Looking at the workload imposed on training and development professionals by the 9-step KPMT model, it is not surprising that this represents a very different role for many, who have traditionally run menus of courses very loosely linked to business needs.

Yet perhaps training and development really is one of the few sources of competitive advantage left to exploit. In fact, if most organisations are as bad at linking their training and development to the bottom line as this report suggests, then those who can start to build in added value evaluation are bound to steal a march on their unfocused competitors.

But if there really is a new, business-focused role for those responsible for training and development, who is going to take on this role? The 'touchy feely' management development 'luvvies', the psychotherapists and neuro-linguistic programmers, the outward bound management schools – or the clear-headed business people who find working in training and development a rewarding career because they can see exactly how to make a contribution?

Skills Development for High-Impact Training and Development Practitioners

If there is a new role to maximise the impact of training and development on the bottom line, what skill sets should such professionals be aiming to develop?

This report suggests that they need to be strategic thinkers and speak the same language as the business. But more than this – they need to be able to translate business imperatives into workable training, development and learning solutions.

The tools and techniques used in this report – together with a full range of business analysis, problem-solving and total quality tools – are all part of a comprehensive toolkit that training and development professionals will need if they are to provide the service that will be increasingly required by all types of organisations.

Appendices

Appendix 1   The toolkit

The simple tools provided here are just a start. If you want to build evaluation into your training and development effort, then many business analysis and problem-solving tools would be helpful. It is well worth, as a starting point, to learn as much as possible about total quality problem-solving techniques.

However, two very important points must be borne in mind:

- Giving you a scalpel does not make you a surgeon. Try these things out gently first, build up your confidence, and keep an open and flexible mind when you use them so that you adapt them to different circumstances.

- Do not try to use a chisel as a screwdriver. Any toolkit has a range of tools, each of which is best suited to particular tasks. Make sure you know what jobs each tool can do and only use them where they are appropriate.

Tool Number 1: Knowing Where You Are in Evaluation

As in any quality improvement programme, there are four stages of evolution along the road towards continuous improvement:

- Unconscious incompetence;

- Conscious incompetence;

- Conscious competence;

- Unconscious competence.

This means that before you start on a quality programme you are not conscious of how badly you are performing (unconscious incompetence). To start to make an improvement, your incompetence has to be fully and openly acknowledged (conscious incompetence). Only then can you move towards consciously improving what you do (conscious competence). Ultimately, using a total quality cycle approach, you aim to get things right first time, automatically (unconscious competence).

So the first step in this process has to be establishing as to how good (or bad) you are at evaluation now. Use the checklist to spot any areas in which your organisation is currently deficient (incompetent).

Pull together all, or just a sample, of the training and development events you run. Assess their effectiveness in evaluation and validation terms as follows:

1.   Are all events linked in some way to the achievement of clear business objectives (KPMT base level)? If not, see Tool Numbers 2 and 3.

2.   Do they all have clear training objectives (i.e. after this event the participants will be able to ...)?

Any that do not must have training objectives defined.

3.   Are any measures of reaction being put in place? If so, this will start to satisfy the Level 1 requirement.

If not, start to produce a reaction questionnaire, but make sure the questions are checking reactions to the event as a learning experience rather than a day out from the office. The most important question is: did the event meet the training objectives set?

4.   How many training events involve any types of test of what the participants actually learned (Level 2)?

   The programmes should be designed to include specific opportunities to check learning throughout. Also, wherever possible, more formal testing should take place. But beware, those who see training as a day out will not always take kindly to being tested on what they have learned.

5.   How many training events involve any system to check that they are transferring what they have learned to their workplace (Level 3)? This could involve:

   - follow-up questionnaires to participants three or six months after the event;

   - feedback from managers or supervisors, both informally as well as formally.

6.   If business objectives have been set, to what extent is evaluation data collected (Level 4)? If there are no built-in measures it is impossible to evaluate the training event in any meaningful way. Move to Tool Number 4.

7.   If evaluation evidence is collected, how is it published and who sees the results?

   - the participants?

   - line managers?

   - other employees?

   - directors?

   - the training department?

   Start to produce some simple, graphical illustrations that training is paying off.

8.   If you fail to follow any of the levels properly, then you now have two basic options:

   - Start at Level 1 and move forward from there, but this will only give you more validation information. It will never answer the Level 4 question.

- Preferably, revisit all your training programmes and question what, if any, business objectives are being targeted. If there are no obvious business objectives, redesign the programmes focusing on business objectives, or remove them from the training programme.

You might also want to try and plot your existing and planned positions on the grid below.

If this tool makes you feel that much of your training is unfocused and unmeasurable then you should now have some idea of the size of the task that you face. Nevertheless you may take some solace from the fact that you and your organisation are not alone in this predicament!

The only other question you now have to ask is: do you really want to improve this situation?

Try plotting where you are now and where you want to be on the evaluation grid in Table A1.1.

What actions would you need to take to move from X to Y to Z?

Table A1.1 Tool Number 1: Evaluation grid – plot your own position

Training/Development: amount and structure

	No evaluation	Some validation of courses	Some validation of courses/ programmes	Evaluation of courses	Evaluation of courses and programmes	Courses and programmes directly linked to business plan
Structured – learning organisation						
Unstructured – learning organisation						
Lots – structured						**Z** – *in two years time?*
Lots – unstructured		**X** – *where you are now*		**Y** – *where you want to be in one year*		
Some – structured						
Some – unstructured						
No training						

Evaluation approach

Tool Number 2: Critical Questioning Techniques

Tool Number 1 will have illustrated to you that maybe the questions you have been asking when carrying out your training needs analysis (TNA) have not been eliciting the sort of responses you need if you are to design business-focused training and development.

Without asking the right questions you will never get the right answers and this will mean that you will waste everyone's time. This is an area in which high-level skills need to be developed. Also, the questions need to be tightly focused and structured.

The sorts of questions that need to be asked are those that:

- identify critical success factors in the business;

- attach measurements to those factors; and

- start to translate those into target areas for improvement through training and development.

Critical questions for the purpose of TNA can be split into three broad categories:

- **Broad business analysis**, to get an understanding of vision, long-term strategy and short-term business targets, parameters and constraints;

- **Diagnosis**, to dig underneath the broad figures and targets in an attempt to identify exactly what problems will be encountered and the root causes of those problems;

- **Prescription**, to establish which causes are directly related to training and development needs so that training and development solutions can be designed to achieve business goals directly.

But, in each case, there should always be an emphasis on questions that are framed in such a way as to elicit a quantifiable answer. It is the quantities expressed that will not only help to focus training and development on the right priorities, but will aid in training and development design, and be used, ultimately, for evaluation purposes.

Here are some examples:

1.   **Broad business analysis** – what are the key issues, constraints and parameters?

What is our turnover, overheads, profit, return on capital? Where do we want each of these to be in two/three/five/ten years' time? Does our current financial position and projections provide a sound basis for this business and, if there are any vulnerable areas or particular pressure points, where are they? What do we expect our competitors to be doing and how much of a threat do they pose to our plans?

What is your department's contribution to the organisation in terms of sales/costs? Which of these measures are you currently focusing your efforts on?

What markets are we in and who are our customers? Are we moving into other markets? What are the size of those markets and what is our market share in each? Have we targets for improvement in each case and what steps are we taking to achieve those improvements?

2.   **Diagnosis** – what is the problem?

If we are looking to reduce costs by 10%, in which areas are we hoping to make these cost reductions and how?

Where will the pressure of these cuts be felt most? If we lose people, who is ready to take over some of their workload?

Of the 10% increase in sales volume, how are we planning to achieve that? Does this figure include any new products and, if so, how much of this percentage will be made up of new products? Will there be an increase in the advertising/marketing budget and what increase in sales would we expect this to achieve? How much of the increase will have to come from increased productivity by the salesforce or are we hoping to improve their effectiveness at selling?

If we are aiming to improve customer retention rates, who are the people in this organisation who are likely to have an impact on customer retention? Should we map out the process (see Tool Number 5) to see exactly who is customer-facing and anyone else who can directly influence customer satisfaction? Who are the ones who offer the best opportunity for improvement through investing in training and development?

3.   **Prescription** – what are the possible solutions?

Say that we have identified from an analysis of complaints data that the vast majority of customer complaints (80%) come from after-sales service. Furthermore, within the after-sales department, 50% of those complaints are simply due to staff failing to give customers a guaranteed date and time for a service call.

Much of this problem is due to the way in which the after-sales department is organised and action needs to be taken to address a more efficient after-sales process. However, there are at least two clear training needs:

- Basic training is required for all after-sales telephone staff on our agreed company procedure to provide customers with a guaranteed date and time. This should immediately reduce complaints in this area by at least 20%.

- The manager and supervisors need to understand where the process is failing. We can arrange a short programme to train them in understanding process analysis to be applied directly to their departmental problems. If successful, this should enable the department to give guaranteed dates and times to all customers.

This series of questions and information gathering is obviously just for illustrative purposes, but the basic principles of good questioning techniques can be learned and continuously honed.

It must be pointed out, though, that for many in the training and development profession there is the added hurdle of asking questions which managers do not expect to hear from trainers. Consequently, there may well be a requirement to become more assertive and tenacious in attempting to elicit from reluctant directors and line managers exactly the right sort of information that is a crucial first step towards effective training and development, delivery and evaluation. But do not forget that evaluation is always a joint activity, a partnership between training and the business it serves.

Tool Number 3: Using Bottom-Line Objectives in Training Needs Analysis

Evaluation can only start from a basis of measuring added value. Added value is the result of bringing about an improvement in a combination of basically four factors – costs, prices, output and quality. Focusing on just one of these without looking at the other variables, simultaneously, will not guarantee value is being added. In other words, there will be no bottom-line improvement.

The simplest example of this point would be seen where costs of production are driven down but quality drops to such an extent that the goods are unsaleable. Added value, therefore, is a holistic measure. If an activity adds value then we can take it for granted that the combination of, often complex, variables is right.

To evaluate training, therefore, the starting point has to be the identification of a clear bottom-line objective which can be influenced by training and development. If the bottom-line improvement target improves after the training and development intervention, we can have some confidence that the training and development itself is playing its part. But how is the link between bottom-line objectives and training and development needs made?

Very simply – a causal connection between the two can be constructed using simple process flow mapping techniques. Take a 10% sales improvement target as an example.

First the bottom-line objective must be an added value objective so we may have to specify that the 10% improvement has to be achieved within a constraint of no increase in costs.

Figure A1.1 shows how there will always be many influencing factors which must be taken into account. The first row of factors would be the major influences and subsequent rows are, in turn, contributors to those factors and ultimately the sales objective. The connections or links do not break down. If they do, the training and development initiative will add no value, no matter how much cost and effort has gone into it.

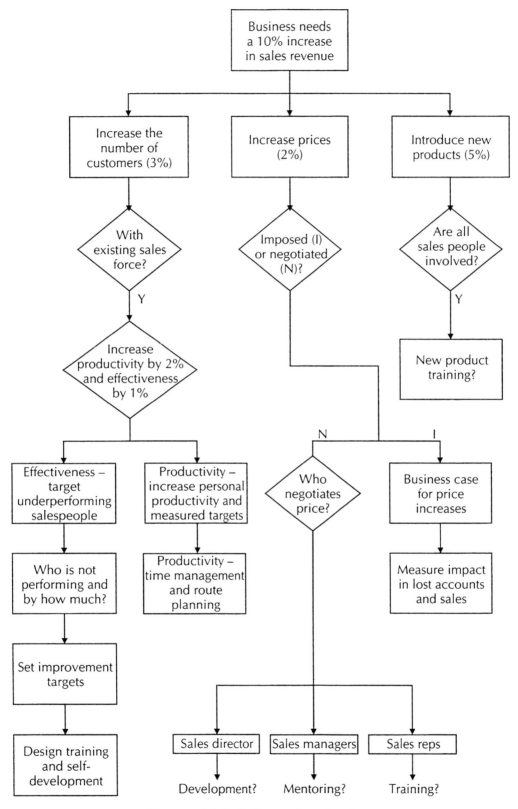

Figure A1.1 Influencing factors.

Tool Number 4: Validating and Evaluating Existing Training and Development

The biggest hurdle for anyone new to evaluation is knowing where to start – especially if applying strict evaluation criteria to current training and development activity indicates that its value is dubious. This tool, therefore, provides a simple approach towards validating and evaluating existing training and development as well as acting as a framework for a longer-term move towards designing all *new* training and development with built-in evaluation.

1.   The first step is to divide all existing training and development activity into three broad categories, using the following table. This can be done by an individual, the whole of the training department or by a selected team representing various parts of the organisation. A few examples are included.

   The first attempt at this can involve as much 'guesstimation' as you wish.

Column 1	Column 2	Column 3
Must have – minimum requirements for the organisation to operate at its minimum standard	**Added value** – this training and development is discretionary, it adds value and justifies investment	**Nice to have** – this isn't absolutely necessary, we have no added value measures but we think it is/might be worth having
Induction	Supervisor development	Leadership courses
Product knowledge		

2.   Now, once all the training and development is allocated, the next step is to look very hard at Column 1. Is this really absolutely necessary for the business to operate effectively? If not, reallocate to another column. If it is, then the next questions are:

   •   how quickly does this have to be delivered?

81

- how can it be delivered at the minimum cost?

- how can we do this training before the 'trainees' are ready to meet the customers or function within the organisation?

This immediately throws up the need to put in place some validation processes for this column (see Tool Number 1).

3.   All the training and development in Column 2 is discretionary. It is not absolutely necessary, but if it is done effectively it will bring with it bottom-line improvements. Some nominal figures have to be allocated to what added value it brings.

Once a nominal value has been placed on it, the next step is to compare the value against the existing cost of providing it. If the return justifies the cost then this training and development can continue, but more effort should now be put into building in real evaluation measures.

4.   Anything which does not justify its cost should be carefully reassessed and perhaps terminated, if appropriate. Anything which is still believed to be important, even without a clear cost/return justification, should be moved to Column 3.

5.   All training and development in Column 3 is highly suspect. The company doesn't need it and its added value is questionable, to say the least. This training and development should be subjected immediately to further scrutiny. Who asked for it and why? Are the recipients of this training and development happy with it? If it fails at any of the validation measures it is a prime target for termination or at least a fundamental review.

6.   What does this exercise reveal? How ineffective is existing training and development and to what extent is training and development investment wasted or unfocused? Start to move towards a two-box model (Columns 1 and 2) using increasingly stringent criteria.

Ultimately, you are aiming for as high a level of confidence as possible that anything in Columns 1 and 2 is providing a level of training and development that the organisation really requires both to keep in operation and to continuously add value.

Tool Number 5: Using Process Mapping for Identifying the Value Adders

A crucial part of making training pay is the ability to identify those people in the organisation who can add the most value. Once these have been identified, and their potential value assessed, then training and development can be focused on achieving the maximum return on investment.

A simple example of this point would be to look at the process of extracting huge pieces of stone from a quarry. The explosives expert, stone cutter and lorry driver all add something to the final value of the stone when it is sold. But if the purchaser happens to be Michaelangelo, the added value soars once he has sculpted the statue of David from it.

Mapping processes is not a new technique but it can be adapted for training and development purposes to extract the maximum value from the people in a process. Look at the simple process flow diagram, or map, shown in Figure A1.2.

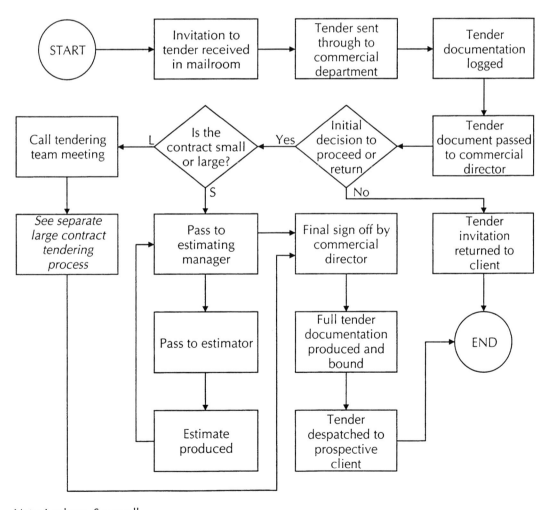

Note: L = large, S = small

Figure A1.2 Process flow diagram for the tendering process.

How can such a map be used in training and development?

1.   First, if it is mapped correctly, it will identify everyone involved in the process: who will be the likely target audience for any training and development needs.

2.   It shows who adds value in the process. In this case it could be the members of the tender team or the individual estimator. Is the training of the team and the estimator enabling them to produce accurate estimates?

      But what value do the commercial director and estimating manager add? If they just rubber stamp the work of the team or estimator, this adds little or no value. Maybe the process should exclude them and they can usefully focus their efforts elsewhere.

3.   At a more basic level, the process map shows how some, apparently insignificant, activities can cause bottlenecks or undermine the final output (i.e. an accurate, commercially sound and professionally produced tender document). Do the mailroom and other staff in the commercial department know how urgent the tender is? Can everyone speed up the time it takes (total cycle time) to produce and despatch the tender? Will the final document be sent out in a clean state with the correct postage and recorded delivery? All of these questions would indicate basic or minimum training requirements.

4.   At a more advanced level, why can't the whole process be streamlined by passing tender invitations straight to the estimator? Are they capable and empowered to make good judgements about what further action, if any, is required? This would reduce the time and cost taken to produce tenders but suggests much broader training and development needs for the estimator.

5.   The 'large contract tendering process' is, in effect, a sub-process of the main tendering process. How clearly defined is it? Do we know exactly who might be co-opted onto it at any time? If not, we could be in serious trouble if someone is asked to take part at the last minute who is not fully trained to play an effective part.

Process mapping is a simple technique. For those who are completely new to it, try 'walking through' a particular process. In this case, this would mean picking up a tender invitation from the mailroom and following it on its journey through the organisation, making notes along the way about who handles the documentation, who has to make decisions and who tends to slow the process up.

The steps involved can then be put on paper in a logical sequence.

Also, note how similar this technique is to that in Tool Number 3.

Tool Number 6: Making Sure It's a Training Problem Worth Solving

This is a relatively simple checklist of sequential steps to ensure that:

- you are designing training and development to solve training and development problems;

- you are focusing attention and effort on an area that is worthwhile for the organisation.

1. **Analyse the problem**

   In addition to using the questioning in Tool Number 2, start to draw a simple cause and effect diagram (see Figure A1.3). Ask the internal customer what problems (effects) they are seeking to resolve through training and development. If they cannot define the effect(s) they are trying to resolve tell them you will return when they can.

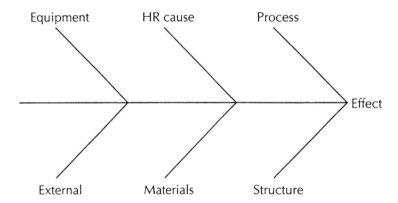

Figure A1.3 Simple cause and effect diagram.

   Let us take, as an example, improving the attitudes and behaviour of ticket collectors on public transport. What exactly is the effect we are trying to resolve – customer complaints, fare dodging or maybe attracting more customers to use that form of transport?

2. **Size the problem**

   As soon as you have an effect put some size on it. 'If we do this customer service training for ticket collectors, how big an improvement might we achieve and how much value is this likely to add?'

Needless to say, if agreeing an approximate size is difficult, this should sound some alarm bells about whether the training and development is going to be worthwhile.

If the size of the anticipated improvement is large, obviously a correspondingly large investment may be required. If the size is small and the issue is not critical, then possibly the focus for training and development should move elsewhere.

3. **Build in a measure**

If we are going to do this training and development, how will it be measured? Whilst there may be a range of measures used, are there any which are particularly objective and directly linked to the bottom-line (e.g. income from fare dodgers)?

4. **Collect the base data**

Although the quick discussion about potential improvement opportunities identified this as an area worth focusing on, we now have to collect some data. Do we know how many tourists use this form of transport and how often they ask ticket collectors for information?

5. **Design the solution**

Only when Steps 1 to 4 have been completed can an attempt be made at training and development design. If the base data suggests that incorrect fares is the biggest issue, then any training and development initiative intended to help could be quite different in content and style to one which addressed the issue of giving tourists clear information on the transport service.

Also, by now, we are able to design a cost-effective solution because we know how big the problem is and how much improvement we are seeking.

6. **Evaluate the outcome**

Despite the view that evaluation is a tiresome, time-consuming task, if Steps 1 to 5 are carried out correctly, the system should now be in place to compare new results with the original measures used at Step 2 (e.g. 'the new customer satisfaction survey indicates an improvement in ticket collectors giving good information, total ticket receipts are up by 5%, and this equates to £X in sales and £Y in profits').

Tool Number 7: Failure Analysis – How to Plan for Success

Whether you try to evaluate training or not, no one wants their training and development programmes to fail. Validation and evaluation can show us where training failed after the event, but do not necessarily tell us *why*. One simple tool which tries to prevent training failure is called failure analysis.

Because everyone thinks training is a 'good' thing to be doing, they rarely stop to take a rather negative stance and consider how it might fail. Yet, in many other walks of life we spend a great deal of our time consciously trying to avoid failure. We arrive at the airport early to make sure we do not miss the flight, we do that last minute bit of revision to give ourselves the best chance of passing the exam.

Manufacturing companies, constantly trying to get it right first time, especially when they may be producing thousands of the same component, need to be absolutely sure that they have anticipated all the foreseeable problems and eventualities, and even a few unlikely ones. Failure analysis is a simple method for spotting possible causes of failure in advance, so that preventative action can be taken *now* to avoid unnecessary cost and production problems.

It is best carried out as a brainstorming exercise with a group which represents those who might be involved in the training process.

Try it out on your appraisal system.

1.   First, you have to define what the objective of the system is – what is its output? There could be a range of objectives including 'improving individual performance'. Once this has been defined, you then have a basis for asking the question 'how might the system fail to achieve this objective?'

2.   The initial list of possible causes of failure can then be produced. This should include any causes which are suggested by the group. As in any brainstorming session, even 'stupid' or 'wacky' ideas are acceptable because the group needs to feel free to explore every avenue.

3.   For appraisal the initial list might include:

        No forms sent out to appraisor.

        No forms sent out to appraisee.

        Appraisee doesn't want to be appraised.

Appraisor doesn't like doing appraisals.

Appraisor isn't trained to carry out appraisals.

Diary dates don't match.

The appraisal interview ends up as a slanging match.

Everyone pays lip service to it.

etc. etc.

4. Now the group has to sift through these to see which of the ideas are very unlikely to happen. These can be discarded.

5. Any remaining ideas now have to be reconsidered and a decision taken as to what avoiding action is required. Responsibilities for taking such actions have to be allocated.

6. The final phase is to produce a plan for introducing or amending the appraisal system with the best possible chance of success built in.

Failure analysis is simple. It should not take up too much time and any time taken is well spent. It can be applied to any single training event as well. It becomes particularly interesting if no clear business-linked training objective has been established.

Tool Number 8: Getting Over the 'Soft' Versus 'Hard' Hurdle

Alongside Tool Number 2: Critical questioning techniques, there is a similar tool required for dealing with the age-old problem of trying to measure or evaluate what are often regarded as soft or intangible issues. This tool is also about asking the right questions but particularly when your internal customers are adamant that the training and development they are seeking is dealing with such factors.

The classic scenarios are those where the board has decided that the organisation is in desperate need of culture change attitude and behaviour change, or improved customer awareness. These views may well be very valid but if this is the only basis for developing a training and development programme it will be one that is unlikely to focus on real added value and, therefore, cannot be evaluated. More importantly, it is therefore unlikely to achieve any change whatsoever.

This tool comes in two parts.

Part 1

First you have to convince your customer that there is no distinction between these so called hard and soft factors. This will normally provoke a response such as 'well what is empathy with the customer then?'

When such a question is asked, the immediate reply is '*why* do we want our people to have empathy with the customer?'

This may lead to 'because we want them to really understand the customers' needs and they need to be able to empathise to do this'.

The next question is the same as the first: 'why do we want them to understand the customers' needs?'

Sometimes the penny drops at this stage. Sometimes it takes a little longer. (Has the penny dropped for you yet?)

Inevitably, it can be pointed out to the person concerned that even the supposedly soft factors are important to the business because they have an impact on perceptions and ultimately on decisions to buy.

If you cannot convince your internal customer of this fact of life you can either decide not to do any training for them or, if you have to, point out that any training will have to be non-business focused, and therefore less likely to succeed.

Part 2

If the customer begins to understand that ultimately there is no distinction between soft and hard, the next step is to ask some questions which convert the soft ideas into measurable business outputs. Again, if there are no obvious measurable business outputs, serious questions should be asked about the reasons for doing the training and development. Is it really a training and development issue or is it another type of problem?

One further hint is that asking someone a straight question does not always receive a straight answer. A sales director may well decide that the main problem with the sales force is lack of motivation. This answer would not provide a basis for action in training and development.

Constantly reframing and probing is one way to get underneath what may well be a very valid view. So questions such as 'do you mean they are demotivated or unmotivated?' and 'are we really saying that the whole sales force is lacking in motivation?' would start to get to the truth. Another useful question is: 'If we could wave a magic wand and sort out your motivation problem, what would we start to see happening – more sales visits, better sales meetings, happier customers or what?' This places the onus on the person using vague language to tighten up their own thinking and start to provide some meaningful information which training and development can use.

Here are some other sample questions which could help.

> 'If the culture of this business changes, how will we know when it has happened?'

> 'If our management believe teamworking adds value, what evidence will we see in a year's time?'

> 'The survey shows that our customers like dealing with friendly staff. Should we invest in "empathy" type attitude training? If we are going to go down that road, how much do we expect sales to rise or complaints to fall?'

> 'If we think it would be a good idea to empower our staff, which of our key business indicators are most likely to improve and by how much?'

But, don't forget, in many cases training will not be the answer or even part of the answer.

Tool Number 9: A Statement of Purpose in Training and Development

Implicit in much of this report is the notion that the role of the training function and/or the training professional will have to change once real evaluation gets underway. If evaluation is about business improvement, then trainers have to become involved in business analysis and more tightly linked to operational management.

This, in turn, will mean that the whole organisation's perceptions of what training and development is and what it is meant to achieve will have to be revisited. The similarities with vision and mission statements in total quality are obvious. Also, the 'commitment' principle of Investors in People addresses this issue.

So, for the training function, there needs to be a clear statement covering:

- the purpose of training and development;

- what comes under the heading of training and development;

- where it is meant to sit in the organisation.

If your organisation says it is committed to business-focused training and development then drawing up a statement which is agreed should not be too difficult. But this is not some meaningless, woolly mission statement. It is something which can be used as a guide for managers and other employees and should help to constantly reiterate the importance of commitment to training and development at all levels in the organisation if it is ever going to be effective and deliver bottom-line results.

Every organisation's statement of purpose will be different, but here are few key elements which should be common to all.

1.   **Training as an investment**

Training and development is an *investment* by the organisation. As such it will be subject to the same, rigorous financial appraisal as all other investments. The cost of the investment will be identified, as will the financial return anticipated. Training and development investments will only be made where the return on investment is acceptable.

2.   **Links between training and development and the business**

All training and development activity will focus on either:

- operational business targets; or

- long-term strategic business objectives.

An obvious and measurable link between training and development and such objectives will have to be clear to trainers, participants and managers before any training and development will be approved.

Tool Number 10: A Simple Checklist Before You Start

Here is a simple list of seven steps that you can use to guide you towards business-focused training and development with built-in evaluation.

1.   Establish the present business situation (effect) that needs improving (you can call this point A).

2.   Can the existing situation be measured or made tangible? If it cannot, then it will not be possible to evaluate any training and development undertaken.

3.   If you have completed steps 1 and 2 then you are in a position to set a measurable improvement target (the desired effect, or point B).

4.   Establish whether training and development can influence, or is one of the potential causes of, the effect A and the solution point B.

5.   Calculate the cost of delivering the training and development solution you have planned.

6.   Consider whether you can get from A to B more cost effectively by a means other than investing in training and development.

7.   Now calculate the expected return on investment (ROI). If it is big enough to justify the planned training and development solution you can now start to implement the training and development initiative.

Appendix 2   Case studies – applications of the tools in practice

These case studies are meant to indicate how the thinking in this report works in practice. They have been kept brief to cover the main principles. In particular, very little detail is given on the actual training methods used as it is the intention to keep focusing on the costing and evaluating elements of the training process. More detailed information can be obtained from the authors.

Case Study 1: Evaluating Empowerment

Stage 1: The Brief

Business process re-engineering had prompted some of the directors to review methods of working and to examine how a more 'enlightened' management environment might enable employees to perform better. The idea that was being pursued involved having a flatter management hierarchy with less direct management supervision.

Whatever was needed, however, would have to bring benefits not only for customers and the business, but also for the staff themselves.

Stage 2: The Design

This was carried out in close liaison with the business director.

Key factors that emerged included:

- a change in supervision ratios from 1:10 to between 1:20 and 1:30;

- reductions in management;

- multiskilling, initially on a trial basis;

- an aim of producing cost savings of £150,00 in year 1.

Another aim was to produce teams of ten employees and produce a system for capturing new ideas and valuing these ideas if implemented.

Based on these discussions, the training design was to introduce:

- empowered teamwork;

- the transfer of certain areas of responsibility;

- a system for capturing, valuing and implementing ideas.

Estimated Costs

An empowerment and team development programme was costed as follows:

	£
Purchase of specific training materials	55,149
Trainees' time (350 people × 2 days × £50)	35,000
Trainers' time and development work (2 × 60 days × £70)	8,400
Management time for small group briefings	3,000
Total	101,549

Estimated payback	
Reduction in management costs	150,000
Reduction in absenteeism levels	Saving expected but not measured
Revised product training in line with teamworking	100,000
Planned return for year 1	250,000

Stage 3: The Contract

These proposals were discussed with the business director, taking into consideration other changes that were taking place at the time. The discussions were particularly lively when the question was raised of how much would be attributable to this particular programme.

What was seen as an area in which the programme would be particularly beneficial was the revised product training possible and the potential creation of improvement ideas.

Management cost reduction would only happen as a result of the programme but no agreement was reached on likely absenteeism improvements.

A programme of implementation was subsequently agreed and measurements would be taken over a two-year period. Full payback on initial costs was expected six months after the completion of the programme.

Stage 4: Training Delivery

The delivery stage was carried out in accordance with the agreed plan and schedule.

Stage 5: Evaluation

	£
Actual costs were calculated at:	101,549

The returns accruing were calculated as follows:

	£
Management savings	50,000
Supervision savings	100,000
Valuations of ideas attributed	198,000
Revised product training over 18 month period	530,000
Total	878,000
Net return	776,451

In addition:

- It was readily acknowledged that absenteeism had also improved, even though this was not part of the contract agreement.

- Staff surveys showed that they enjoyed working in teams and measurable evidence showed productivity improvements.

- Customer satisfaction monitoring also showed improvements which was an indication of staff attitudes at work.

Stage 6: Feedback

Data was fed back to the business director who was pleased with the overall benefits. This case study has been evaluated by a number of organisations and has been separately investigated and reported on in other management literature.

Case Study 2: Improving Productivity Through Training Using the KPMT Six-Stage Model

Stage 1: The Brief

In 1992 the business user had a requirement to increase individual productivity in his particular area of the business. The request was for 'something' that would improve performance. A 5% increase was being sought in the overall plan.

Stage 2: Design

A casual observation of the group of employees concerned revealed that they were using keyboards for a significant amount of time per day. The average time on the keyboard per employee was about 2.5 hours per day.

They had received no keyboard training previously and there were no keyboard tests at the recruitment stage. A subtle observation of a sample of the group revealed that not only were they slow but they were also making significant mistakes which they were correcting.

Suggested Method

To design a business keyboard system (not a typing course) which would replicate the business environment whilst measuring pre and post training results. In addition, the payback needed to cover all training costs. Initial observations indicated that there was an opportunity for performance improvement in this area to justify training investment.

Breaking Down the Costs

Testing out the simple assumption that training could pay off, the following figures were produced:

		£
Number of staff to be trained	166	
Amount of training required	16 hours per person	
Staff cost per hour	7.24	
Total staff salary costs		19,229.44
Trainers'/manager's time	37.9 days	
Cost of time per day	£70	
Total trainers' cost		2,653.00
Equipment and new software		34,000.00
Total costs excluding overhead recovery		55,882.44
Training on-costs @ 18%		10,058.84
Total		**65,941.28**

Stage 3: Agreement and Contract with the Business User

Based on the outline cost figures, a view was taken on what productivity and accuracy gains would be achieved. The benefits from these gains would accrue through planned business growth without a corresponding growth in keyboarding operators. In hard cash terms this was converted to a cost saving of £130,000 per annum.

Furthermore, this meant that the initial payback period for recouping costs would be approximately six to nine months.

Following on from agreement to proceed on this basis, a further discussion took place to cover the methodology and training times in more detail, as well as methods for measuring improvements.

Stage 4: Delivery

This was the relatively easy stage. The training was delivered on time to the agreed plan, using the automated delivery system and some proprietary software.

Stage 5: Evaluation

Pre-course information had been gathered by the training system, giving 'before' and 'after' training results.

> Average speed had improved from 5,555 to 9,060 key depressions per hour.
> Accuracy had also improved from 89.5% to 96.4%.

Converting these improvements into time savings (26 minutes per person per day on average) and then cost savings resulted in an **annual benefit figure of £635,112.03**.

Stage 6: Feedback

Pre and post results were explained to the original business manager requesting the training, together with a summary report of how the figures were arrived at. All of the data was hard, with no allowance for subjective interpretation.

Case Study 3: Achieving Sales Improvement Through Telephone Sales

Stage 1: The brief

The main business need was defined as measuring call quality in a structured way. This was intended to increase sales per person by 8% in what was already regarded as a well established and well trained workforce.

This would be added value training to help gain a competitive edge.

Stage 2: Design

A great deal of time was spent in researching possible avenues to explore and a lead from the marketing department helped to locate a possible source of unique material from America.

Also, experience in measuring the soft and hard competencies would help to establish a methodology for measuring the quality of each telephone call, if necessary.

Breaking Down the Costs

		£
Divisional training director's time on researching		3,000
Training costs:		
Materials		97,000
Staff training time	60 × 3 days × 80 people	14,400
Trainers time	100 × 50 days	5,000
Total costs		119,400

To provide a baseline for estimating a payback figure, a measurement exercise was completed to establish exactly what the average sales figures were, over a 20-week period. In addition, a further discussion took place with the business customer to fully understand the variables that might affect results.

Calculations on payback suggested that successful training could result in improved quality of calls, improve sales by up to 10% and gain a competitive edge for approximately 18 months.

Stage 3: Agreement and Contract with the Business User

The contract agreed with the business customer covered:

- material costs (which required board approval);

- the measurement methods to be used;

- the timetable;

- checking the other influencing variables.

The only variable of concern was the freeze on recruitment which would mean that anyone leaving after they were trained would have an impact on results. Unfortunately, this point was not negotiable.

Payback time was agreed to be over a two-year period, although the training director was confident that full payback could be achieved in less time.

Stage 4: Delivery

Performance advantage training started and followed the agreed programme. It was not well received by the staff who were convinced that their performance and quality standards could not be improved.

On-site coaching by trainers and line managers took place immediately after training. All measurement systems were in place to record progress.

Stage 5: Evaluation

Skills were measured on a 12-point scale – each point could achieve a mark of 10 if it was being carried out perfectly. Instant and direct feedback was given at the time of measurement.

Little improvement in sales was apparent for the first four weeks but then this situation changed dramatically. After week 11 the weekly increase in sales, based on the original baseline figure, never fell below 25%.

Stage 6: Feedback

Feedback on the results was very well received by the customer but other areas of the business were sceptical as the results were so good. Various studies have further validated the results, including an independent study carried out by the Institute of Personnel and Development in 1995. Details of this were reported in their *Measurement of Training Paper Number 11*.

Case Study 4: Measuring the Payback Periods for Existing Training Investment

Introduction

This is a short case study where some of the principles espoused in this report were applied to existing training and development. It is based on a short project carried out in the leisure sector. Although there was significant investment in training and development this was the first time that anyone had tried to show what effect it was having on the bottom-line.

The company had a business plan to grow the business significantly over a three-year period. Much of this growth was to be achieved by opening several new branches each year.

Each branch would be in a different part of the UK and there would be a recruitment and training campaign to ensure the branch was ready for business on schedule.

In the wider market, though, many new competitors had entered the market and this had imposed significant pressure on margins. As a defensive measure, the company had taken a serious look at its own cost structures and had taken cost out of new branch openings by reducing project planning and building costs.

When opportunities in these areas had been exhausted, an obvious target for savings was the significant recruitment and training budget, despite the fact that this company believed its training investment to be critical to the business and money well spent.

The Challenge

The training manager, under pressure to save money out of the training budget, asked the simple question: 'How can I ensure that we still deliver the standard of training we require and save money at the same time?'

The Variables

An apparently simple question posed a particularly complex problem. A discussion took place to establish exactly what the important measures, factors and variables were. The main ones which needed to be focused on to answer the question were regarded as:

1.   The average recruitment and training cost per person.

2.   The return on this cost, which would be dictated by three main factors:

- the time/cost taken to train individuals up to the minimum standard required to work in a new branch (1,200 per head);

- the value then generated by each individual (profitable sales);

- the length of time for which they are employed (in order to payback their training costs).

The Project

A short project commenced to produce some clear, practical measures which would help to answer the question posed by the training manager.

What became obvious was that:

1.   Training was seen more as an input than an output. The amount of initial training covered in the two-week standard training programme was considerable and many new starters could not handle it. This impacted on staff turnover and delivering the 'input' was no guarantee that it was converted into 'output' (the retention of knowledge and development of skills which deliver customer service), even though post-training tests were carried out.

2.   Many of the staff concerned were paid on a commission basis and very accurate measures of performance were available, in bottom-line terms.

3.   Although the company was very concerned about its high staff turnover (averaging 90% per annum), branch managers did not seem to want to own the problem or manage it in any meaningful way. Indeed, they tended to see it as an unavoidable part of their business.

The Solution

1.   The concept of training according to how much individuals can absorb and assimilate in a relatively short time, was revisited.

Certain 'total coverage' aspects of the training content were trimmed.

2.   Calculations were carried out to translate the commission data into individual, added value contribution figures. This showed that an average performer would have to be employed for 38.5 weeks in order just to recoup (payback) their own initial recruitment and training costs.

3.   Measuring turnover was not ensuring that the problem was being managed effectively and the real problem was that, not only was there a high staff turnover, but a high proportion of it was very short term indeed (especially in the first three months of employment). Therefore, a definite move to stability measures was made (i.e. the number of employees with more than six or 12 months service at any particular point in time). Once the branch managers were told that they 'lost money' on most of the staff who left within 38.5 weeks they were happy to accept stability improvement targets based on this figure.